INTRODUCTION TO EDUCATION
Series Editor: Jonathan Solity

PUPIL BEHAVIOUR AND TEACHER CULTURE

BOOKS IN THIS SERIES:

PUPIL BEHAVIOUR AND TEACHER CULTURE

Andy Miller

CASSELL

Cassell
Wellington House   127 West 24th Street
125 Strand   New York
London WC2R 0BB   NY 10011

First published 1996

British Library Cataloguing-in-Publication Data
A catalogue record for this book is available from the British
Library.

ISBN 0-304-33684-X (hardback)
      0-304-33683-1 (paperback)

Typeset by Action Typesetting Limited
Printed and bound in Great Britain by
Biddles Ltd, Guildford and King's Lynn

CONTENTS

Part 3: Assigning Responsibilities

Part 4: Implications for Future Research and Practice

ACKNOWLEDGEMENTS

This book has drawn on the time, enthusiasm and encouragement of many people. A large number of teachers and educational psychologists gave significant amounts of their time in order to take part in interviews and complete questionnaires. Without their help this study would have been impossible and I am extremely grateful to them for their co-operation and their example of professional commitment. Their identities, and those of the pupils and parents, have been protected by the use of pseudonyms.

I am particularly indebted to Dr David Thompson for his supervision of the research project which led to this book and, with all the usual disclaimers about the responsibility for remaining weaknesses, I would like to acknowledge the support and critical advice given by Gerv Leyden, Jayne Nash and Jonathan Solity during the writing of this book.

For John Thacker

CHAPTER 1

Introduction: perspectives on pupils' behaviour

For the last quarter of a century at least, the idea that the behaviour of pupils in schools is becoming more unruly and uncontrolled has never been absent for long from newspaper reports and political discussion. As Gilham (1981) observed, 'There was a point in the early seventies when it seemed as if many secondary schools in the major urban areas were heading for breakdown.' Teachers, parents, pupils, communities, employers and politicians all have a perspective and these become picked up, intertwined and widely dispersed by the forceful gusts of public opinion. And within all this concern, there is a danger that the rhetoric will further inflame anxieties and undermine a belief in the potential of professional problem-solving, collaborative action and sensitively targeted research.

There are many legitimate questions generated by this public concern. Are children becoming more out of control? Are some parents abdicating their responsibilities? How far have new teaching methods and philosophies been responsible for any changes? Can schools change and can they make a difference? Have schools been deprived of adequate funding and teachers undervalued by governments and society at large? Is there too much professionalization of education? Are there too many experts or are there too many armchair philosophers? Have

1

research and theory complicated basic issues or have they unearthed levels of complexity that must be addressed in a society undergoing massive change?

All of these questions, and others, deserve answers. For some of them, research studies have provided definite, and for others tentative, clarification. For some people, however, no amount of empirical evidence will displace passionately held convictions, beliefs that may derive from a professional lifetime of open-minded curiosity and reflection or be held with equal conviction as a result of casual contact with some of the more lurid tabloid newspaper headlines. Instead of taking questions such as these one by one and attempting to provide answers, this book will begin with a set of personal anecdotes.

At the base of my 80-year-old father's left-hand little finger is a white scar of about half a centimetre in length. It is the result of his being caned across the hand at 7 years of age on his first day at junior school. A senior member of the staff had entered the classroom all those years ago and asked him an arithmetical question. Because his answer was inaudible, he was summoned to the front and instructed to extend his left hand. When I first heard this story as a child and inspected that permanently whitened line of skin, I seethed with anger at the injustice. He, on the other hand, has borne little malice.

In the mid-1960s, I lived for a while in a hall of residence attached to a teacher training college. Meetings in this all-male establishment frequently decried the lack of 'standards' that were perceived to characterize the wider student body within the college. One night a fellow resident had an intense and sudden religious conversion and would subsequently proclaim loudly and indiscriminately about his spiritual upheaval. In a small kitchen area on one of the floors, a few evenings later, a group of about fifteen trainee teachers blocked the doorway and goaded on a craft and design student as he beat up the new convert.

On the first day in my second teaching post I asked a 10-year-old boy to sit down and he gripped the sides of his table, fixed me directly in the eyes and grinned, with all the unrestrained mischief of a puppy ready to play. In my first post I had been seen as a successful teacher and discipline had never been a consideration. As my previously effective demeanour and manner failed to bring about any control, a growing sense of excited anticipation rippled around the other members of the class. Drawn to contemplating chasing the boy around his desk, and the almost inevitable débâcle that would ensue, I felt very alone.

In the past few years I have worked with a primary school staff and the parents of a boy who, by the age of 6, had been excluded from one previous school and removed from a second before the same thing could happen. In his 'last-chance' third school, this little boy's difficult behaviour has been slowly replaced by a positive and enthusiastic response. Nearby, in a secondary school, a team of teachers have maintained in mainstream schooling a boy who has experienced tragic early life circumstances. His bizarre and unsettling behaviour has reduced considerably and the time-consuming individualized planning carried out by his teachers has improved his chances with a range of public examinations and prevented his removal to a special school where his opportunity for contact with the full range of adolescent social behaviour would have been denied. Stories of very young children being excluded from, or refused entry to, schools and of teenagers seemingly out of control make for dramatic headlines in the press. The existence of these successes, on the other hand, has registered nowhere beyond the minds of those who have been directly involved.

The point of these personal anecdotes, which are hopefully more than an indulgence, is to suggest that the behaviour of pupils in schools is a subject which is not easily reduced to a few pragmatic questions. Instead, these diverse examples hint at the large and untidy set of issues involving authority and control, justice and fairness, rationality and emotion, the conditions for optimism, the effects of peers, the professional socialization and potential isolation of teachers, and the influence of personal experience and recollection itself. In order to advance discussion, this chapter will introduce a structure. But author and readers alike should bear in mind that beneath the order and progression lies a set of complex ethical, philosophical, psychological and social themes, often ill-disciplined in themselves, ready always to chase around the table the proponents of both the easy answer and the logical and detailed analysis.

One way of beginning to structure the discussion about pupil behaviour is to recognize that historically at least two very different approaches have been taken. One has concerned itself with what might be called the craft of the teacher in terms of classroom management or control. Another very different strand of thinking has grown up around the study of the 'problem child'. Interestingly, these perspectives have traditionally had very little to do with each other, the former often existing at the level of staffroom folklore and the latter deriving from varying theoretical positions.

This chapter will briefly describe each of these perspectives and illustrate their influences upon legislation and government advice to schools concerning the management of difficult pupil behaviour. The contents of the remainder of the book will then be briefly introduced.

CLASSROOM MANAGEMENT

The Elton Committee, in its report *Discipline in Schools* (DES, 1989), found a fairly common belief among teachers that group management skills were a 'gift' and that teachers were either 'born with them or not'. After pursuing this line of enquiry through teacher training institutions, local education authorities and surveys of teachers, the committee concluded

> First, that teachers' group management skills are probably the single most important factor in achieving good standards of classroom behaviour. Second, that those skills can be taught and learned. Third, that practical training provision in this area is inadequate. (p. 70)

Traditionally, research into this area has taken the form of empirical studies in classrooms using various structured observation methods. Galvin and Costa (1994) have reviewed some of the most significant of these studies and concluded that

> The classroom management research movement has identified a wide range (almost too wide) of factors that can reasonably be considered as the basis of good classroom management practice. Room layout, classroom routines, managing transitions, maintaining momentum, curriculum issues, managing groups and getting the year off to a good start are just a few of the key areas of preventing misbehaviour from occurring in the classroom. (p. 146)

SCHOOL EFFECTIVENESS

Supplementing the studies of classroom management has been the body of investigation usually collected under the title of 'school effectiveness' research. This has shown that the standard of pupil behaviour as well as academic attainment can vary between schools, irrespective of a school's catchment area, and can be partly influenced by factors within a school's control.

Although Reynolds (1992) has pointed out that the research on 'social outcomes', such as the behaviour of pupils, is not as advanced as the work linking school processes to pupils' academic progress, none the less studies have certainly indicated likely influences. Some of these factors were identified by Rutter *et al.* (1979) in their influential study, *Fifteen Thousand Hours*. By examining 12 London secondary schools in detail, this research suggested that, among other things, 'effective' schools had common policies on behaviour, made consistent use of rewards, created a pleasant working environment and paid careful attention to issues of classroom management. Another major British study by Mortimore *et al.* (1988) focused upon 50 London primary schools and identified 12 school factors that were related to school effectiveness, mainly again in the form of pupils' academic achievements. One set of these factors, such as purposeful leadership by the headteacher, represented school-level processes, whereas the other, which included record-keeping, might be characterized at both a school and a classroom level.

Although school effectiveness research is becoming more and more widely promulgated, Reynolds (1992) provides a salutary reminder that this work has been highly contentious and that, after very early work that found delinquency rates varying considerably between schools (Power, 1967, 1972), the researcher in question was refused access to schools for further investigations.

THE 'PROBLEM CHILD'

Whereas the Elton Report reflected the growing practical implications of the school effectiveness and classroom management research literature, and encouraged schools to adopt or extend their practice as organizations, a continuing paradox continues to surround the notion of the 'problem' or 'impossible' child (Lane, 1990). Obviously, the pupil whose behaviour is so challenging, pervasive and unresponsive to all that teachers appear to have to offer will make a major impact on those responsible for his or her education. And yet the more extreme the problem, the more likely it is that professional groups outside mainstream education – those in psychiatry, psychology, social work or a separate special education system – will be seen as the appropriate bodies to provide an explanation for this behaviour and/or effect a solution.

Lane (1994) has reviewed the range of theoretical perspectives that have been employed in an attempt to account for difficult pupil behaviour and has shown how these have influenced different types of professional responses. He considers the roots of the child guidance clinic movement within psychoanalytic traditions and the later attempts, mainly by psychologists enthused with the promise of the early research studies into behavioural approaches, to use these approaches more directly in their work with schools. In a wide-ranging review, Lane also considers the extent to which explanations involving congenital, family, neighbourhood, sub-cultural and cultural factors have been utilized and the extent to which they have contributed to practical intervention measures. He also examines social processes such as discrimination and labelling.

Nobody could argue that unsupported teachers should be solely responsible for managing the most extreme behaviour of a very small minority of pupils. But a case could be made that, by separating off expertise into agencies outside schools, teachers are less likely to acquire knowledge, skills and confidence that might be of help to them in their work with slightly less challenging pupils who none the less stretch their professional capabilities. And, in some ways, by not acquiring expertise for those levels of problems, the pattern is then able to repeat itself, with a less practised professional response being available for the next gradation of lesser seriousness, and so on.

Clearly, the issue is one of drawing lines – between the reasonable and the unreasonable, the feasible and the impractical, the unsupported initiative and the complete transfer of responsibility. Put more specifically, how far can school processes be expected to extend down to meet the most extreme challenges presented by pupils in mainstream schools and how far into the total body of pupils should non-educational 'problem child' explanations and professional responsibilities extend?

LEGISLATION, CATEGORIES AND THE DRAWING OF LINES

Recently, the British government has issued a series of circulars to schools (DFE, 1994a, 1994b, 1994c) offering advice on just these issues. Basically these documents posit a spectrum of children who might display difficult behaviour:

- children who are 'disruptive or naughty', or experiencing some emotional stress within normal and expected bounds;
- children whose symptoms are those of a serious mental illness, the occurrence of which is rare;
- children with emotional and behavioural difficulties, who lie on a spectrum between these other two groups and should be construed as having some form of learning difficulty.

'disruptive or naughty', some emotional stress, normal and expected bounds	emotional and behavioural difficulties	a rare serious mental illness

The circulars avoid over-simplistic categorizations and attempt to offer advice based upon research studies and professional opinion of the type discussed above. For instance, the first category of pupil is seen as the responsibility of the school and class teacher and associated recommendations draw on the research into school processes. Circular 8/94 (DFE, 1994a) states that 'individual instances of disruptive behaviour are bound to occur at times' and that, in response, 'interventions have to be carefully judged by teachers, using their knowledge of individual pupils or class groups'. These teachers should do 'no more than is needed to secure the desired change in the pupil's behaviour'.

At the other end of the spectrum, the grouping of pupils with a 'serious mental illness' is described as being very small but consisting of 'young people (who) develop severe emotional and behavioural disorders which require care and treatment beyond that which can be found in school, including special school' (DFE, 1994c). Children characterized in this way 'may be referred to a unit, often on a residential basis, because they have exhausted the resources or the ability to cope of their community, family and school and require an environment which can facilitate cognitive and emotional growth' (DFE, 1994c).

The third grouping, the children with emotional and behavioural difficulties, are likely to have a persisting problem which constitutes a learning difficulty. Such a view conceives of difficult pupil behaviour as arising primarily either from an inadequate repertoire of socially desirable behaviour or from the learning of unacceptable methods of responding to certain social demands, especially those encountered within school settings. As a form of learning difficulty, emotional and behavioural difficulties should be met via the stages of assessment and intervention set down in the 1993 Education Act's *Code of Practice on the Identification and Assessment of Children with Special Educational Needs* (DFE, 1993).

Much of the tenor of the descriptions of these categories suggests that the qualities of the children are relatively fixed and likely to be manifested across a range of contexts. Perhaps this is less so for the first group, the pupils who are 'disruptive or naughty within normal and expected bounds', where there is an implication both that this state of affairs may well be transitory and that mainstream teachers can exert a significant influence over its future direction. Construing emotional and behavioural difficulties as a *learning difficulty*, however, carries a more definite message that the problem exists with and 'within' the pupil. But even here, Circular 9/94 (DFE, 1994b) acknowledges that external factors can be implicated not only in the definition of such difficulties but in their possible maintenance, amplification or amelioration:

> Perceptions of whether a child's behaviour constitutes an emotional and behavioural difficulty are likely to differ according to the context in which it occurs as well as the individual teacher's management skills, tolerance levels, temperament and expectations. (DFE 1994b)

The category of children with a rare 'serious mental illness' certainly seems a less ambiguous entity, at least at first sight. For children in this category, the 'problem child' paradigm immediately transfers the responsibility for making sense of the difficulties outside education and into the realm of medical diagnoses and explanatory mechanisms. Whilst this is clearly and entirely appropriate in the cases of children and young people where a definite physiological, neurological, or hormonal mechanism is at work, it can be more questionable for other types of diagnosis originating from a psychiatric perspective. The problem is not that these perspectives are 'wrong', but that they give an unequivocal message, not necessarily intentionally, that the difficulties are lodged deeply and totally with the pupil.

Controversies still exist about the extent to which a number of psychiatric 'illnesses' do have an environmental component. Clearly, a common-sense view would be to ensure that, with any children who might appear to merit this type of description, multi-professional liaison and co-operation must be of the highest order. Gray and Noakes (1992) have detailed the complex of reasons why very different professional perspectives such as medicine and education can be so hard to reconcile in the case of difficult pupil behaviour. It is obvious that teachers do not have a medical training but it can be less obvious to those outside education (and less easy for some within to admit) that individual teachers' 'management skills, tolerance levels, temperament and expectations' can vary and have some effect upon pupils' behaviour in schools.

At this stage in such a discussion, some may begin to despair. Reducing the apparent argument to a stark example, they may ask whether it is being implied that the most vicious or anti-social acts by children, perhaps committed well outside the school premises, are going to be swept away by a gesture such as the pupil being allowed to wash out the paint pots – the fairy's kiss school of ivory-towered expert opinion. This is not what is being suggested.

There are empirical as well as anecdotal grounds for suggesting that schools and teachers can, with or without the support of others, move pupils some distance along the DFE's spectrum – in either direction! How far? Sometimes only a small distance, at other times a whole category or even more. There is not necessarily anything completely fixed or immoveable about pupils' behaviour and the major disadvantage of thinking too much in categories is the consequent strong implication that there is.

Later in this book we will examine in detail case studies of successful collaborative work between teachers and educational psychologists. What shall we say of the infant school deputy headteacher who was wound to such a pitch by a small boy's behaviour that her family life began to deteriorate and she questioned whether she could continue to work as a teacher? How far down the spectrum of seriousness was that little boy's behaviour? And how far along the spectrum had he travelled if, after a period of sensitive collaborative work, this rejuvenated teacher could say 'I can honestly say that he's not like the same child'?

THE CODE OF PRACTICE

The other recent major government initiative, as mentioned above, has been the 1993 Code of Practice. Within this, schools are required, via class teachers, to identify children with special educational needs and make an appropriate class-based response. If this proves ineffective then teachers are to consult with the school's special educational needs co-ordinator, who should make a further assessment of the pupil's difficulties and further suggestions about methods for supporting the pupil in class. A third stage is then reached, if these still prove unsuccessful, whereby schools supplement their own skills with those of support services outside the school. In the case of children with emotional and behavioural difficulties, these outside agencies are most likely to be behaviour support teachers and educational psychologists. Subsequent stages, if the pupil's difficulties are still resistant to intervention, allow for 'statutory assessments' which may then lead on to local education authorities (LEAs) issuing Statements of Special Educational Needs. These may then recommend the provision of additional resources or an alternative placement for the pupil.

The procedures laid down in the Code follow a clear pattern, and criteria for record keeping and suggestions for early-stage interventions are given. Although these can form a structure for professional action, the Code can do little to influence many of the untidy and powerful processes referred to earlier in the anecdotal illustrations. For example, a teacher who feels defeated, less competent than colleagues, or exhausted, is unlikely to embrace enthusiastically suggested strategies, simple or complex, from close colleagues or relative strangers. And if teachers have reached a point where they have little or no sympathy for a pupil who has made their life a misery, then the *sine qua non* for any intervention – not the whole intervention but one essential ingredient, a positive and valuing approach – will be unavailable. Going through the motions, with any of these typical emotional reactions present, will only lead to rapid progress through the stages, supplemented by a dossier of failed interventions reinforcing a picture of the pupil's position as irredeemable. While the Code and sensitive professionals are anxious to avoid feelings getting to this pitch, the power of difficult pupil behaviour to get deeply under the skin of teachers in a relatively short time should not be underestimated.

As indicated above, the present book gives detailed examples of successful interventions at what are effectively stages 3 and post-5 of the Code, although the research actually took place just before the formal implementation of this piece of legislation. One of the major findings from the research reported here is that teachers do not pass these interventions on to colleagues with similar pupil difficulties. They are, in fact, extremely reluctant to discuss them in the majority of cases, despite often experiencing a major turnabout in a problem they had judged to be the most difficult they had encountered in their whole careers! Many of the teachers also describe feelings of debilitating isolation in respect of the difficult pupil, despite the existence in many cases of school-wide behaviour policies and colleagues on the staff who are generally perceived as a supportive group of people. In the light of such evidence, things do not augur too well for the Code of Practice, at least in terms of successful and professionally satisfying work with difficult pupils being easy to accomplish in the early stages. There seems to be more to the successful management of difficult pupil behaviour than even the most comprehensive and well structured set of guidelines can fully hope to address.

THE SCOPE OF THE PRESENT BOOK

This book is about successful interventions at the primary school level. It takes as its starting point the successful use by educational psychologists (EPs) and primary school teachers of what are usually known as 'behavioural approaches'. It is not, however, a book primarily about behavioural approaches. They are in effect the vehicle – perhaps even the Trojan Horse – for access to a range of processes, such as the effects of teacher cultures, the emotional consequences for teachers trying to manage difficult pupil behaviour, the styles of thinking about these difficulties often employed by teachers and the contentious issue of parental responsibility. The major theme of the book is the way in which behavioural approaches impact upon real schools as organizations, illuminating and engaging these social processes.

The term 'behavioural approaches' is redolent with connotations. For some it may be rats in mazes and psychologists in white coats. For others, it is bribery, coercion or an unjustly tolerant attitude towards disobedience and disorder. For others again, it is the one tune of the remote and unworldly visiting 'expert' with star charts and smiley faces spilling from his or her arms.

It doesn't have to be this way. There is a large and well-documented set of research papers showing that successes can sometimes follow from these approaches, with the implication that a completely dismissive attitude would not be a fully professional response. Many recent developments – the emphasis on clear rules, rewards and sanctions in school behaviour policies, and popular training packages such as *Assertive Discipline* (Canter and Canter, 1992), *The Behavioural Approach to Teaching Package* (Wheldall and Merrett, 1985), *Preventative Approaches to Disruption* (Chisholm *et al.*, 1986), *Building a Better Behaved School* (Galvin, Mercer and Costa, 1990) and *You Know the Fair Rule* (Rogers, 1990) – all draw, to a greater or lesser extent, on the research and practice base developed in individual behavioural interventions with pupils.

The first section of this book takes a close look at what is happening with behavioural approaches in Britain. Chapter 2 provides a brief outline of the major characteristics of these approaches by describing the first experiment in this area and then drawing upon the research literature to pick out a number of the key themes and controversies that have subsequently developed. Because it is often only the highly successful case studies that find their way into the academic journals, Chapter 3 presents the results of an investigation into a wider set of interventions taking place outside the limelight. It looks at the results of a national survey into the actual details of interventions devised by EPs and teachers. Finally in this section, in an attempt to learn important lessons for the implementation of the Code of Practice, Chapter 4 looks at what teachers find to be the disadvantages and unattractive features of these approaches.

Teachers often report feelings of isolation when faced with challenging behaviour on the part of a pupil or pupils in their class. Researchers and external consultants such as EPs, when working with individual teachers on such concerns, have tended to lose sight of the fact that these teachers are all located within schools – systems with their own rules, cultures and patterns of social interaction. These themes are explored in detail in the second and third sections of the book, Chapters 5 to 10. Readers for whom these topics are of greater interest may wish to start the book at this point, although approaching the chapters in the conventional fashion should give greater coherence to the overall picture. These readers may wish to return to Chapters 2, 3 and 4 after their preferred sections.

The methodology adopted for the major section of the research, the detailed analysis of the accounts by 24 teachers of successful interventions, follows a grounded theory procedure. The purpose of such a methodology is to generate theory, to attempt to *explain* by reference to a wider body of theoretical literature and to add coherence to a set of otherwise disconnected and disparate phenomena. Not everybody is happy with theory. There are some who, in John Major's words, would like to 'understand less and condemn more' and they may wish to omit Chapter 12. However, a deeper understanding of a phenomenon obviously does not mean that a greater tolerance of unacceptable acts must therefore follow. And it is a deeper understanding of phenomena that has given us, for instance, penicillin and landed men on the moon, or curtailed our burning of women as witches. For those whose concerns are of a mainly pragmatic nature, however, Chapter 12 may be subjected to a more cursory approach. Finally, another brief concluding chapter brings the discussion back to some of the contemporary themes raised in this opening chapter. With research informed by the concerns of practitioners, and practice informed by appropriate research activity, we must be in a better position to make progress in this area which continues to be difficult and demanding for education professionals.

PART 1

IMPROVING PUPILS' BEHAVIOUR

CHAPTER 2

Successful interventions with difficult pupils: issues in behavioural approaches

In the previous chapter, the claim was made that a range of influential training materials had their origins, at least in part, within the study and practice of applications of behavioural psychology in educational settings. A similar influence may be found within much of the recommended reading prescribed by the Elton Report and again, more recently, within the notions of targets and behaviour management strategies that form part of the procedures within the Code of Practice.

Behavioural approaches have therefore clearly exerted an influence upon major developments within policy and practice, although they have also retained a controversial reputation. A number of published accounts give a clear exposition of behavioural approaches within British educational contexts (for example, Westmacott and Cameron, 1981; Harrop, 1983; Wheldall and Merrett, 1984; Cheeseman and Watts, 1985; Bull and Solity, 1989). Assuming that readers either already possess a familiarity with the topic or are able to consult these introductory texts, this chapter will present only a brief introduction. In order to give a flavour of a number of basic characteristics and demonstrate historical roots, the first major published study of behavioural approaches within education will be described and used as a springboard for outlining subsequent controversies and developments.

In the original study of Madsen *et al.* (1968), carried out in American schools, the researchers were concerned to illustrate the major tenet that behaviour is learned and that pupils can thus learn acceptable and productive classroom behaviour. The experiments show a concern with clearly defined and observable behaviour rather than assumed personality characteristics and motivations of pupils. The careful collection and recording of data, often in graphical or tabular form, is another key feature which is conspicuously present in the study. This attention to the clear presentation of data serves the very important function of allowing those concerned with interventions, especially the children, to have unambiguous information about how the strategy is progressing. Finally, behavioural approaches are structured around the principles that behaviour is governed by the settings in which it occurs (setting events) and by what follows it (consequences). Setting events, or antecedents, can comprise a whole range of educational, social and physical factors (see Table 2.1) and in this study are prominent in the form of the clear exposition of classroom rules. Consequences, on the other hand, are present in the study as contingent praise and the ignoring of specified behaviour.

THE PIONEERING STUDY BY MADSEN AND COLLEAGUES

The first published study consisted of accounts of helping three pupils improve their classroom behaviour. Two of these children were in the same middle-primary classroom and the other in a kindergarten class. The behaviour of this latter little boy was characterized by his teacher when he entered the class as 'wild'. He would 'push and hit and grab at objects and at children. He had no respect for authority and apparently didn't even hear directions. He knew how to swear profusely. He would wander round the classroom and it was difficult to get him to engage in constructive work. He would frequently destroy any work he did rather than take it home.'

The study not only attempted to bring about positive changes in these pupils' behaviour, it also attempted to employ a strict methodology in order to demonstrate the nature and extent of these changes. Consequently, as this was a research project, two observers were trained over a two-week period to make precise records of the pupils' behaviour in the classroom. A set of categories of inappropriate behaviour was devised and confirmed with the class teachers concerned. Nine different categories of inappropriate and one of appropriate behaviour were described. The former consisted of gross motor movement, object noise, disturbance of others' property, contact, verbalization, turning around, other inappropriate behaviour, mouthing objects and isolate play. This last category was included because observations were to take place during structured group activities and playing alone would then be seen by the teacher as 'inappropriate'.

Each of these categories was then split into a number of precisely-worded and observable behaviours. For example, the category 'verbalization' was elaborated to include: carrying on conversations with other children when this is not permitted, answering the teacher without raising a hand or without being called on, making comments or calling out remarks when no questions have been asked, calling the teacher's name to get her attention, crying, screaming, singing, whistling, laughing, coughing, or blowing loudly. These responses might have been directed to the teacher or the children.

The appropriate behaviour category was defined as 'answers questions, raises hand, works on assignment. Must include whole 10-second interval except for Turning Around responses of less than 4-second duration'.

It is important to stress here that the aim of the experiment was not to reduce or eliminate every aspect of inappropriate behaviour, with these massive lists being put before a five-year-old child like the labours of Hercules. These definitions were for the observers only, the purpose being to allow a very precise and detailed record of pupils' behaviour to be kept over the experimental period. For this reason, some definitions were made with such a high degree of specificity as to appear ludicrous on first sight if their purpose is not appreciated. For example, 'turning around' was described more explicitly as 'turning head or head and body to look at another person, showing objects to another child, attending to another child. Must be of 4-second duration, or more than 90 degrees using desk as a reference ... '. And so on.

The emphasis on such a detailed list of inappropriate behaviour also gives a misleading impression of the major aim of the project, which was to increase the amount of appropriate behaviour on the part of pupils during specific classroom activities. The more detailed list served an important function, however, in that it provided a greater number of items and thus increased the sensitivity of the observations. Because of the fairly exhaustive nature of these categories, if inappropriate behaviour was shown to decrease then this could reasonably be assumed to be a result of an increase in appropriate behaviour.

The purpose of the study was to investigate experimentally the effects on pupils' classroom behaviour of teachers varying their use of praise, ignoring and the explanation of rules. For the purpose of the experiment, the teachers were asked to adopt certain procedures for formulating and explaining classroom rules to the children in their classes. These were to be no more than five or six in number, short and to the point, and framed in a positive rather than a negative form (for example, 'sit quietly while working' rather than 'don't talk to your neighbours'). The teachers were asked to keep a tally sheet on their desks and record the number of times they reviewed the rules, aiming for at least four to six repetitions each day, at times other than when somebody had misbehaved.

The second phase of the experiment involved ignoring inappropriate behaviour unless this was leading to a pupil being hurt. The reason for this phase of the experiment was to test the possibility that inappropriate behaviour was being strengthened in some cases by the attention being paid to it by the teachers, even though this was intended to act as a punishment. Perhaps not surprisingly, the teachers in the study found this a particularly difficult strategy to implement and sustain as an intervention on its own.

The third phase, the praise condition, was framed as 'catching the child being good'. The teachers were asked to give praise, attention or smiles when the pupil was doing what was expected during the particular class in question. The teachers were also encouraged to 'shape by successive approximation', starting by giving praise and attention to the first signs of appropriate behaviour and working towards greater goals. Emphasis was to be placed on positive and helpful social behaviour and following group rules. The general principles were to give praise for behaviours which facilitated learning, to tell the children what they were being praised for, and to try to encourage behaviours incompatible with those to be decreased.

Figure 2.1 shows the proportion of inappropriate behaviour displayed by the kindergarten pupil during different phases of the experiment. The baseline period consisted of a record of the pupil's behaviour before the introduction of any of the three experimental conditions – rules, ignore and praise. The observers kept a record of five 10-second intervals in every minute over a 20-minute period on three occasions each week. The percentage of intervals in which *any* inappropriate behaviour occurred was then graphed over the various sessions. Thus the higher the scores on the graph in Figure 2.1, the greater the amount of inappropriate behaviour, and almost certainly the lower the amount of appropriate behaviour.

Figure 2.1   Inappropriate behaviour of one problem child in Classroom B as a function of experimental conditions
From Madsen *et al.* (1968)

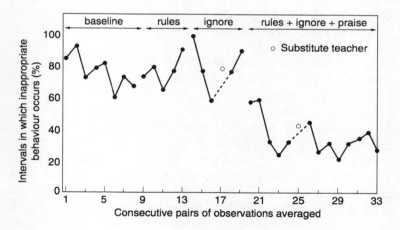

When the experiment began, the teachers were trained in the use of each phase before recording took place and were asked to apply these to the whole class, not just the target pupils, and for the whole time rather than just the observation periods. In the primary school observations took place during seat work or group instruction and in the kindergarten class during structured activities rather than free play. Two observers were present in each classroom in order to check the accuracy of each other's recordings ('inter-observer reliability'). The teachers and the pupils were reported to learn quickly not to respond to the observers (although one of them was attacked by a kindergarten child!) and the experimental recording did not commence until the two observers had settled into a pattern of consistent agreement in their recordings.

The results for the two pupils in the primary class were similar to those from the kindergarten setting shown in Figure 2.1. As this illustrates, the rules and the ignoring phases on their own produced little change from the baseline condition but the combination of rules, praise and ignoring proved highly effective in reducing inappropriate behaviour.

From this relatively detailed account of the first published study of behavioural approaches, it has been possible to illustrate many of the major characteristics of the behavioural approach. The effect that altering antecedents and consequences can have upon the ability of pupils to learn new ways of behaving in classrooms has been demonstrated. Likewise, the precise descriptions of behaviour have allowed careful records to be kept in graphical form, thus giving the pupils, teachers and researchers clear feedback that the strategy had achieved its aims.

KEY ISSUES IN THE DEVELOPMENT OF BEHAVIOURAL APPROACHES

The study by Madsen and his colleagues created considerable interest among professionals with a direct responsibility for helping teachers manage the difficult behaviour of some pupils. In 1971, Ward repeated the experiment in a Manchester school with similar results and published the first British replication of this work. A major reason for the early growth of interest in behavioural approaches derived from the concern placed within the approach on the careful collection and recording of data. Results such as those in Figure 2.1 provided clear evidence that teachers could affect the behaviour of some of the most difficult pupils in mainstream primary schools. This optimistic prospect was in strong contrast to the then dominant trend of 'patho-logizing' difficult pupils, either as fixed deviant personality types or as members of families or subcultures immutably hostile to the efforts of the educational establishment. Behavioural approaches, on the other hand, because they emphasized the role of learning, enabled pupil behaviour to be seen as situation specific. So, although schools were not necessarily in a position to compensate for a range of social factors, the approach did encourage the belief that teachers could have an effect upon the behaviour of pupils whilst they were within their charge.

However, although behavioural approaches soon attracted a group of professionals keen to extend the research base and to proselytize among the wider educational community, they also managed to generate a considerable degree of controversy, oppo-sition and hostility. Some of this resistance stemmed from limitations within the original formulations of the approaches, whilst other misgivings might be seen more as a reaction to a partial appreciation of the nature of the methods themselves. The remainder of this chapter will deal in a little more detail with some of the major developments that have taken place in an attempt to overcome early weaknesses in practice and meet the misgivings and apprehensions from professional quarters.

The over-reliance on consequences

In the minds of many who came upon behavioural approaches, an overriding emhasis came to be placed upon the rewards and punishments that followed pupils' behaviour. Although antecedents, in the form of clear explanations of rules, were prominently contained within the Madsen *et al.* (1968) study, the focus of immediately subsequent work was very much upon the consequences of behaviour. The terms antecedents and setting events are used interchangeably in this discussion, although this has sometimes produced confusions in the litera-ture. It is not necessary for the purposes of this chapter to distinguish between the two, although a very useful clarification can be obtained by consulting the paper by Wheldall and Glynn (1988). Antecendents were generally not considered to be suffi-cient on their own to have a significant impact on some behaviour, whereas consequences were seen as much more likely to determine whether or not a behaviour was strengthened and maintained. It was this view that became most firmly associated with the term 'behaviour modification' – a term which has fallen from use with the continuing evolution of methods.

Two of the earliest British proponents, Harrop and McNamara (1979), took stock of their practice after a five-year period of gathering casework and group workshop experience with teachers using behavioural methods. They commented on their move towards giving greater emphasis to classroom rules, as well as praise and ignoring. They made the point that behavioural interventions had to ask whether the curriculum within the classroom where the difficult behaviour was being manifested should be altered to meet the pupil's interests and aptitudes before embarking upon a fuller behavioural intervention. Similarly, Wheldall (1981) pointed to the dangers of what he termed 'behavioural overkill', the use of very powerful reinforcers to change behaviour where a less powerful and more 'natural' reinforcer would suffice. He was also another who stressed that behavioural approaches needed to take the focus away from the consequences of behaviour and place it more upon the antecedents.

Pursuing this line, Wheldall *et al.* (1981) carried out an experiment with two classes of 10- and 11-year-olds in a junior school. The amount of 'on-task' behaviour was recorded over a two-week period while the children were seated around tables, the measurements then being repeated for a further two weeks while the children were seated in rows. The mean on-task behaviour was higher for the rows condition and when the children were subsequently returned to tables for a further two weeks, their mean on-task behaviour declined. Examination of the data revealed that the rows condition had the greatest effect on the children with low initial on-task behaviour, the very pupils for whom behavioural interventions were usually devised.

Although this study might be seen as contributing to discussions about classroom layout, its relevance here is as an early experimental demonstration that contingencies – consequences delivered following the occurrence of specified target behaviours – are not the only factors that can bring about changes in classroom behaviour. And although experiments in such areas as classroom layout need not necessarily originate with proponents of behavioural approaches, it could certainly be argued that the methodology developed within the behavioural paradigm, especially the recording of pupil behaviour, enables or at least encourages them to be conducted.

Bradley and McNamara (1981) also called for greater attention to be paid to antecedents by referring to work in a school for what were then termed 'maladjusted' pupils. They suggested that such factors as the geography of the classroom, the routine order of the day and the classroom rules should always be considered in behavioural interventions. McNamara (1982) cited an example of a failed intervention in which the teacher of a class of third-year juniors had been unable to implement a 'rules, praise and ignoring' approach. Looking at the intervention in retrospect, McNamara stated that, had he paid a greater initial attention to antecedents, he would have realized that the class was very poorly organized and would not have attempted to implement a contingency approach.

This change of emphasis to include the possible triggers to pupils' behaviour, and the setting conditions in which they occur, has become incorporated into the standard texts on the subject but has probably not altered the 'carrot-and-stick' caricature of behavioural approaches firmly lodged in some sections of the public mind, as well as in the understanding of some education-based professionals.

The focus upon 'on-task' pupil behaviour

Following on from the study by Madsen and his colleagues, many subsequent publications about work in primary schools and some special school settings consisted of case studies also concerned with increasing the 'on-task' behaviour of pupils. With the steady accumulation of accounts of practice, some psychologists began to voice misgivings about the general direction of such work. Surveying the American scene, Winnet and Winkler (1972), for instance, cautioned that the current thrust of behavioural approaches in classrooms at that time could be summed up in the injunction to pupils to 'be still, be quiet, be docile'.

In a similar vein, McNamara and Harrop (1981) commented

on what they saw as the 'waves of development' of behavioural approaches in Britain, and concluded that until the early 1980s much practice had been 'somewhat naive' in focusing so much attention upon 'on-task' behaviour as opposed to 'academic work output' and other skills and socially acceptable behaviour. They argued that if behavioural approaches were to move beyond encouraging what might be only a superficial pupil compliance, a lot more attention would also have to be paid to manipulating such aspects of the setting events as lesson preparation.

As a result, a far greater number of subsequent studies switched their focus to include a greater emphasis on academic work output and on encouraging the development among pupils of a range of new skills. Developments such as these were driven by the recognition that pupils who were more able to succeed at conventionally valued school work were more likely, as a result, to identify more closely with the aims of the school and receive more naturally occurring praise and encouragement for their efforts.

Central features of the behavioural approach such as stating clearly-defined target behaviours, task analysis (splitting tasks and targets into smaller steps) and recording schedules have also been adapted for a far wider set of educational and social purposes. Burland (1979), for example, described work in a school for pupils with emotional and behavioural difficulties in which behavioural principles were rigorously but creatively employed to teach pupils a range of social and leisure skills – everything from juggling to riding unicycles! In addition to introducing an element of fun and getting away from the image of behavioural approaches as being always aligned to control and conformity, this work had a serious intention. Not only did it display the versatility of the approaches, but for a group of children with underdeveloped social skills and restricted friendship groupings these new talents became a source of satisfaction in themselves and a probable entry into a wider social acceptability.

Reviewing the first decade of developments in British educational establishments, Merrett (1981) described studies that had been successfully employed to help pupils with a range of problems as diverse as temper control, school refusal, extreme nervousness, peer rejection and memory difficulties. Creative applications of the approaches had moved a long way beyond encouraging the uncritical compliance and docility feared by early commentators.

Applications beyond the individual pupil

Extensions of the techniques also moved beyond working with individual pupils displaying difficulties to inform the practice of teachers in managing whole classes of pupils. The first British experimental validation of the behavioural approach's positive contribution to management of a whole class was provided by Tsoi and Yule (1976), who used extra break time as a reinforcer. Two types of strategy were each shown to be effective, one where the behaviour of a single child formed the basis for reinforcement for all the class and one in which changes in the behaviour of the whole class were required. The study was well designed and thus able to demonstrate objectively the experimental effects.

Merrett and Wheldall (1978) employed a similarly rigorous methodology in a study that was again concerned with management of the whole class, in this instance combining a 'rules, ignore and praise' approach with a 'timer game'. Basically, this involved a teacher using a cassette tape prepared so that it gave a random signal on average once a minute. On the signal, target children were observed and house points were awarded to all the children on the target child's table if he or she was following the set rules. Merrett and Wheldall (1987) commented that 'no teacher would want to use such a device often, or for long periods, but it remains a very useful strategy for gaining, or regaining, control of a group of children who display difficult and/or disruptive behaviour' (p. 28). Rennie (1980) subsequently employed other game strategies with whole classes, again with success.

Whereas much of the discussion in this chapter concerns interventions which aim to help pupils who present management difficulties to their teachers, there have also been developments of a more proactive and preventive nature. Bull and Solity (1989), for example, drawing on the lessons learned from the research into behavioural approaches, have provided detailed guidance on classroom management to enable teachers to maximize the learning of all pupils in a class by reducing the possibility of difficult pupil behaviour arising in the first place.

In an influential set of resource materials, *Building a Better Behaved School*, Galvin *et al.* (1990) pulled together the research on effective classroom management to combine the principles from behavioural studies with those from other areas of research. In addition to influencing individual pupil management techniques and whole-class strategies, this publication and the Elton Report (1989) also drew attention to the crucial importance of establishing clear and mutually agreed policies within schools for encouraging positive pupil behaviour. Again, principles from the behavioural literature, including the earliest emphasis on clear statements of rules and appropriate rewards and sanctions, were incorporated centrally into these recommended whole-school policies.

Generalization

Clearly, an intervention that demands much in terms of the time of a teacher and psychologist would show relatively little return for this effort if its effects were to last only as long as the most intensive application of the intervention. Consequently, practitioners have shown an enduring interest in the issues of treatment generalization, or the extent to which improved behaviour is maintained and spreads after the ending of the intervention. Five possible forms of generalization can be envisaged.

Improved behaviour by the child generalizes beyond the intervention to other settings

Presland (1981) outlined twenty-four suggestions that might aid generalization of a pupil's changed behaviour. Drawing on the research literature, he included among his suggestions: involving other children in providing reinforcement, involving the child in the construction of the programme and explaining to the child how improvements can be transferred to other behaviour and then encouraging these.

A little later, Gurney (1987) demonstrated, by means of a small-scale controlled study, that behavioural approaches could even be effectively employed in an area of interest traditionally seen as diametrically opposed in its focus – the area of humanistic psychology concerned with raising self-esteem. In this study pupils were taught, using contingent reinforcement, to make more positive statements about themselves and display more overt behaviours related to high self-esteem and, upon subsequent testing, were found to have internalized these and to be displaying a higher level of generalized self-esteem. In terms of the potential to aid generalization, proponents of humanistic approaches would predict that pupils with increased self-esteem would be likely to display less difficult behaviour in a range of settings.

Improved behaviour in the target child influences the behaviour of other children

A few studies have measured changed behaviour in pupils other than the pupil who was the target of the particular intervention. Harrop (1978b) demonstrated measured improvement in the classroom behaviour of two 15-year-old boys in what was then a school for ESN(M) pupils, when a third pupil in the class became the recipient of a standard teacher-administered behavioural intervention. The details of the programme were not communicated to the other two pupils by the teacher. Harrop argued that, although the pupil probably discussed these contingencies with his friends, as these friends were not themselves rewarded another type of explanatory mechanism was required.

He speculated that a form of modelling of desirable behaviour may have occurred, or that the reduced disruptiveness of one pupil may have led to fewer opportunities for the same type of behaviour from others, or that seeing one pupil receiving more praise from the teacher may have stimulated the others' desire to seek the same. Harrop could not be certain of the exact mechanism responsible for this phenomenon and concluded that 'just how this happened leaves considerable room for speculation'. It certainly is the case, however, that children in the early years of primary school do achieve an understanding of strategies used by teachers with individual pupils, even when details are deliberately kept from the rest of the class (Miller, 1996).

Leach and Byrne (1986) demonstrated similar 'spill-over' effects of improved classroom behaviour on to 'equally disruptive control students' in a study of a home-based reinforcement scheme in an Australian secondary school. They argued that it was important to attempt to identify possible facilitative factors so that spill-over effects could be explicitly planned for and encouraged.

The term 'generalization' has usually referred to the behaviour of pupils who were the subjects of interventions, although a case can be made for extending the concept to include the behaviour of teachers.

Changed teacher behaviour towards the target child extends beyond the intervention

McNamara (1977) was one of the first to raise the question, based on his early experiences with behavioural approaches, whether all teachers wished to change their behaviour in the direction required by these interventions and, even if they did, whether they would all be able to.

Little in the way of data has been collected to provide an answer to whether teachers persist in the use of some or all of the procedures in a recommended strategy beyond its designated duration. Some teacher behaviours could become habitual and not consciously exercised, whereas other teachers might think they were still following certain recommendations when in fact they had deviated markedly from them – a phenomenon known as *treatment drift*. In neither sets of circumstances would teacher reports be very reliable sources of data for judging whether or not teachers continued to use aspects of interventions.

One empirical source is the Teacher–Child Interaction Project (Berger *et al.*, 1987) which was an extensive attempt to train teachers in the use of behavioural approaches and then evaluate their application. Although it was not possible to demonstrate statistically significant changes in teachers' classroom behaviour, the trends were in the direction predicted. There was a 'striking' within-group variability among the small number of teachers studied, but an interesting 'sleeper effect' was discovered whereby teachers changed their behaviour more in the predicted direction some time after the cessation of the project rather than immediately afterwards.

Changed teacher behaviour extends to other pupils

Presland (1978) followed up twenty-seven teachers who had attended his workshops on behavioural approaches and found that seventeen reported that they were using some of the techniques with pupils other than the study child. There is also a suggestion, of course, from Harrop (1978a) and Leach and Byrne (1986) that two of the teachers in their studies generalized their new management techniques to some or all of the other pupils in the class.

Target teacher influences the behaviour of teacher colleagues in directions related to the strategy

Although there have been published accounts of whole-school approaches to using behavioural strategies in special schools (e.g. Burland and Burland, 1979; Fry, 1980), there have been no published accounts of teachers in British primary schools influencing colleagues after taking part in a behavioural intervention. The special-school staff who published these accounts worked at establishments that had a reputation for using such approaches and catered for what were known as 'maladjusted pupils', where a special interest in behaviour management would be expected.

Presland in his early workshops for teachers made assiduous attempts to gauge the extent to which a ripple-like spread of new ideas could be expected within schools. After providing a course for six teachers from ESN(M) schools in 1977, Presland reported that although on follow-up four out of five were trying some of the techniques with other children, 'it seemed unlikely that their expertise would spread rapidly to other teachers'.

In a larger, more specific, investigation the next year Presland (1978) found that only five respondents out of twenty-seven had influenced anyone else to use the techniques and one of these was in a special school where other staff were required to join in work with the target child. In fact, 'there were no clear accounts of influence leading to effective applications' and, Presland concluded, 'nor is there any support here for the hope that [course] participants might pass on the approaches to colleagues in an effective way'.

These studies suggest that practitioners have been concerned from an early stage in the application of behavioural approaches to understand more fully the conditions for maximizing generalization of the effects of interventions. Although the issue remains complex, there are good grounds for concluding that various forms of generalization are attainable and that some of the necessary precursors have been identified.

Control and autonomy

Finally, the perception that behavioural approaches are inevitably bound up with the desire to *control* has been particularly persistent in some quarters. At the time of the earliest studies, the *Zeitgeist* within education was strongly in terms of 'child-centredness'. Whatever forms this ethos actually took in practice, central aspects of the rhetoric at least included: a curriculum built around children's interests and varying abilities; teaching methods that aimed to encourage and support learning rather than teach directly; and a room layout and timetable organization constructed around the principle of maximum flexibility. All of these sat uncomfortably alongside the widespread perception of 'behaviour modification'.

Interestingly, at the same time, behavioural approaches were gaining widespread credibility among psychologists working with an adult population in various clinical settings. By experimenting with creative adaptations, a range of adult problems and disorders as diverse as eating disorders, sexual dysfunction and agoraphobia were ameliorated. Techniques that were devised all retained the central characteristics of the approach outlined at the beginning of this chapter – the notion that behaviour is learned and that new behaviour can also be learned, the focus on setting events and consequences, the clear definitions of target behaviours, and the careful recording of precise information. However, these approaches, which came to be classed under the title of 'behaviour therapy', did not suffer from the same connotations of control as their educational counterparts.

In fact, employed in a clinical context, behaviour therapy was in many ways far more 'democratic' and open than many of the 'talking therapies' with which they were in competition for professional acceptance. Whereas the latter were usually constructed around the premise that the therapist had greater insight into the client's problems and would decide how much of this to reveal as part of the treatment, behaviour therapists were to be found asking clients to be actively involved in planning and implementing the strategy – from determining target behaviours to changing antecedents and administering their own chosen consequences and recording schemes. In educational settings at the time, behavioural approaches retained a stronger aura of control, perhaps by being allied to the inevitable, if sometimes unvoiced, need of schools to create and maintain a degree of order among their pupils.

Moves towards pupils having a more autonomous role within strategies came about as the result of attempts by some practitioners to extend the benefits of behavioural approaches to secondary school teachers and their pupils. This was generally found to be a far harder undertaking than similar work at the primary level. McNamara and Harrop (1979), for example, found that when they attempted to repeat for secondary staff the types of workshops that had generally proved welcome and successful for primary teachers, there was a much reduced benefit. Following a course for 100 probationary secondary teachers, there was only a limited response, compared with primary teachers, in terms of accounts of successful interventions supported by accompanying data. They concluded that these results, and the general paucity of studies in behavioural approaches in secondary schools, could mean that these schools did not easily lend themselves to such approaches.

A clear example of work at secondary level was provided by Wheldall and Austin (1981), who had persuaded the headteacher of a comprehensive school to carry out a rules–praise–ignore intervention with a fourth-year class identified as difficult by the staff. Using a signal of a random bleep, the headteacher was asked to make a judgement on whether the class was adhering to the particular four rules used in the study and, if so, to award a point which built into a system of free time for the class. From a baseline of 55 per cent on task, the intervention achieved an increase to a 95 per cent rate. Although McNamara and Harrop (1981) gave this study a 'cautious welcome', they argued that the involvement of the headteacher showed how hard it was to enlist the efforts of the school staff in the intervention.

Previously, McNamara (1977) had offered a set of suggestions as to why working with secondary schools might be more problematic. These covered aspects of the organizational complexity of large schools and considerations of the older pupil-group involved, for whom teacher praise might not in itself be reinforcing in the same way as it was for younger pupils, and might in fact have the opposite effect.

In order to overcome some of these factors and make the benefits from behavioural approaches available at the secondary school level, an interest grew in methods whereby pupils were responsible for monitoring and reinforcing their own behaviour. An early account was provided by McNamara and Heard (1976) of an experiment in a secondary school in which some of the beneficial effects of self-recording were demonstrated. Lane (1977) also provided case history examples of successful work carried out from a clinic base with two secondary-aged pupils, one with a reading difficulty and the other with a problem of controlling outbursts of temper.

A clear account of a detailed study of a pupil self-control strategy was provided by Merrett and Blundell in 1982. They reported on work involving a 13-year-old boy in what was then termed a remedial department of a comprehensive school, who displayed a very unsettled approach to many aspects of his work and also distracted other class members from theirs. Following a baseline period, an intervention was introduced which required the pupil to tally his on-task behaviour during the same periods that his teacher collected a similar record. A signal, audible to both the pupil and teacher, was used to indicate when both should record the behaviour. It was explained to the pupil that only the tally marks of his that agreed with his teacher's would be counted towards a reinforcing activity – ten jointly agreed marks could be exchanged for a 2-minute period of colouring-in a Doodle Art picture. The boy's on-task behaviour rose from a mean level of approximately 30 per cent during the baseline period to a mean level of more than 60 per cent during this intervention period.

An interesting 'reversal' design feature was then introduced whereby the pupil did not record his own behaviour but continued to earn reinforcement as a result of his teacher maintaining the same recording schedule. His on-task behaviour fell to a mean level of 40 per cent during this period and then rose again to 61 per cent when the full intervention was reintroduced. A 6-week follow-up, after the cessation of the intervention, in which the teacher repeated the original baseline measures without the pupil being aware of this, showed that the rate of on-task behaviour was being maintained at a high level.

Subsequently, Panagopoulou-Stamatelatou (1990) reviewed the research carried out at primary level in mainstream schools on attempts to train 'children to be responsible and, thus, have the ability to maintain and alter their own goal-directed behaviour'. She looked at studies aimed at improving pupils' academic skills, others concerned with pupils' classroom behaviour, more specifically 'attention-to-task', and those that were a mixture of the two. As a result of her analysis of the published literature, she was able to conclude that

> Self-management procedures have often proved to be powerful in changing classroom behaviours by means of increasing children's appropriate or decreasing inappropriate social behaviour, as well as improving their academic behaviour.

Finally, Houghton (1991) provided a detailed Australian case study in which a 6-year-old pupil learned a self-monitoring strategy by means of 'a high degree of teacher management'. The boy was described as being 'intellectually impaired' and exhibiting disruptive classroom behaviour. His time was spent between a mainstream class and a 'support classroom' and, by teaching the self-control strategy in the support class, it was possible to record a decrease in disruptive behaviour in both settings and at follow-up one week after discontinuing the strategy.

In addition to reducing the aspects of control of pupils and increasing the extent to which they take responsibility for their own behaviour, this trend towards self-control strategies can also be seen as another attempt to encourage generalization by reducing the pupils' reliance upon externally delivered reinforcement.

From this discussion of significant themes, it is possible to see that the cruder stereotypes of 'behaviour modification' have not reflected the diversity and creativity within developing practice. Rather than being over-concerned with control through the excesses of artificially-introduced reinforcement schedules, practice has in fact encouraged teachers to take a more reflective stance towards pupil behaviour. The approach addresses the educational, social and physical environments and therefore has the potential to inform a comprehensive conceptualization of the difficulties both experienced and presented by some pupils. Table 2.1, for instance, taken from Bull and Solity's (1989) book, demonstrates the degree to which the lessons derived from research into behavioural approaches can be incorporated into good practice in general classroom management.

Table 2.1 **Examples of physical, social and educational setting conditions**

Physical factors	Social factors	Educational factors
Amount of space for working and movement	Group sizes and composition	The type of educational task, its relevance, difficulty and length
Seating arrangement	How children are to work: together/alone, etc.	Teacher's presentation and instructions.
	Classroom rules	
Distribution of materials	Teacher's behaviour towards individuals and groups	Written instructions and examples
Noise levels	Children's behaviour towards each other and teacher	The pattern of activities across the lesson and the day

Source: Bull and Solity (1989)

The early stereotype of an over-concern with controlling the 'on-task' docility of pupils through the heavy-handed use of punishments and rewards, if it ever existed to any significant degree, should have been largely dissipated by the growth of practice. The interest in classroom and school environments as setting conditions, the attention paid to matching pupils to educational objectives, and the reality behind the stereotype of a creative and optimistic attitude towards teachers and difficult pupils, have all made an impact upon the wider educational scene. Most of all, perhaps, the feedback obtained from the collection of detailed data has allowed teachers to examine their own contributions to pupils' behaviour and gain a clear sense of achievement in circumstances that sometimes demand the highest levels of professional competence and commitment.

With their roots in the search for a scientific understanding of the ways in which schools might help their most challenging pupils, many of these developments have led to a renewed interest in the physical, social and educational environments of schools and classrooms. However, practitioners are now also in a position to draw directly on the lessons learned from studies of work with individual pupils as they attempt to meet the requirements laid down in the *Code of Practice* for individual educational plans. From this research base, the potential exists for the construction of justifiable, responsive and effective programmes of action.

THE GAP BETWEEN RESEARCH AND PRACTICE

This chapter has quoted extensively from the research literature in an attempt to understand better the ways in which teachers may increase their skills in managing difficult pupil behaviour. But what if this research is not typical of the circumstances in which teachers and EPs find themselves for the majority of their time?

In order to be sure that suggestions and recommendations are widely applicable, it is necessary to supplement these accounts with a study which seeks to find out the spread, take-up and outcomes of behavioural interventions across a large number of practitioners. McNamara (1988) claims that published demonstrations of the successful use of behavioural interventions 'have often been carried out under conditions that maximise the probability of a successful outcome.' Yet these may only have a limited resemblance to the contexts in which EPs often work when a pupil is exhibiting disturbed classroom behaviour. In such circumstances teachers may be more anxious, feel more under threat, less informed and amenable to new concepts, and more interested in interventions that provide extra resources or remove a difficult pupil – that is, in accelerating the pupil through the stages of the Code of Practice.

The everyday work of an EP frequently suggests that devising behavioural programmes that teachers will actually implement involves consideration of a whole range of issues not normally addressed, or at least not given a central position, in a literature that concentrates mainly on either the principles behind programme planning or examples of the successful applications of such programmes. Rather than exploring a small set of 'sparkling successes', the next chapter will therefore look at a national survey of the use of behavioural approaches, including partial successes and failures, in order to arrive at a fuller understanding of practice not just within the 'demonstration study' but also in the more troubled contexts in which teachers and EPs frequently attempt to pursue their collaborative endeavours.

CHAPTER 3

A survey of the use of behavioural approaches in primary schools

In order to gain a more accurate picture of how strictly the behavioural approach was being applied outside the more conducive setting of the 'demonstration study', a survey of practising LEA EPs was carried out. Its main aims were to provide a description of what was actually being delivered by British EPs in the name of behavioural approaches, how effective this was, and whether certain aspects were more or less essential for any success that was being achieved. It was also hoped that a more detailed description of professional practice would yield a set of suggestions to aid the planning of effective individual educational plans aimed at pupils' difficult behaviour.

THE SAMPLE

In order to gain a clearer impression of the actual nature of the programmes EPs are devising for, or in conjunction with, teachers, a questionnaire was devised. All the EPs in 13 randomly-selected LEAs in England and Wales were sent a pre-questionnaire asking whether they ever employed behavioural approaches and would be willing to complete a longer questionnaire on the subject. The pre-questionnaire was thus an attempt to establish some form of prevalence rates as well as identify probable respondents to the major questionnaire. One hundred and forty-seven EPs, 63 per cent of those sampled, returned this pre-questionnaire.

A particular context and set of behavioural problems were chosen for study. Questions were restricted to programmes designed for mainstream primary classrooms, because the body of practice within secondary schools is less developed. Similarly, it was judged that in special schools and units there might be a greater familiarity with behavioural approaches and this would lead to a different type of teacher and EP consultation. An attempt was also made to define the type of children's behaviour under consideration.

In essence, EPs were asked about programmes for children described as either restless, unsettled, completing little work, engaging in physical attacks on other children or not being compliant with teachers' requests or instructions. This was an attempt to shed more light on work done with that group of children often described as disruptive, troubled or troubling, rather than those who had various learning difficulties but remained relatively 'well-behaved' in the classroom. Completed questionnaires were ultimately received from 68 EPs, representing a response rate of 64 per cent from those who had expressed a willingness to participate.

THE QUESTIONNAIRE

The questionnaire was mainly structured by listing as inclusively as possible sets of possible components of a behavioural intervention. Additional questions encouraged more detailed replies by asking for expansion of certain items.

Respondents were asked to answer each item from two separate perspectives, one with their last recommended intervention in mind and the other with their typical practice in mind. Clearly, EPs would be likely to give replies that reflected well upon their practice, either by choosing an intervention in which they had achieved successful outcomes or, at the least, selecting one in which they had performed conscientiously. The first attempt to minimize these effects was to emphasize in the covering letter that the study was trying to obtain a picture of typical practice. It was stressed that respondents should answer with their last intervention in mind, irrespective of whether or not they considered it to be detailed or brief, or whether it had proved successful in its outcome.

The second check on this potential bias was the inclusion of the opportunity to offer equally detailed information on typical interventions. Thus it was made more acceptable to describe a less than complete or successful last intervention when it was also possible to rectify this immediately by indicating that it may not have been typical practice.

RESULTS

The pre-questionnaire

The 147 EPs who responded to the pre-questionnaire represented 63 per cent of the personnel of the 13 LEA services randomly selected for the study. Assuming that these services are representative of the national picture, it is possible to draw some conclusions about the prevalence of the phenomenon under investigation. How often in England and Wales, in one year, do EPs and teachers devise some form of behavioural intervention for these types of problems in primary schools? Is it in the tens, the hundreds, thousands, tens of thousands, hundreds of thousands, or what? What order of magnitude is being discussed? (Asking EPs these questions informally before giving them the results of this part of the study has certainly produced a very wide range of 'guesstimates'.)

If the 63 per cent who completed the questionnaire were the *only* ones in their services to be using these approaches and this was a typical proportion in any service, then the number of interventions devised in one year can be estimated by multiplying the average of these respondents' estimates of the number of interventions per year by the total number of EPs in England and Wales and then by 63 per cent. This yields a minimum figure of around 12,500 interventions per year in England and Wales.

Of the 147 respondents, 15 per cent stated that they did not use such approaches. By including all the missing replies in the 'user category', a maximum figure of around 21,000 programmes per year can be calculated, although the actual figure is likely to be closer to 12,500 because of the tendency of non-responders to be less enthusiastic about the subject matter of a questionnaire.

This figure of 12,500 still suggests that a considerable body of experience in consulting with teachers over behavioural interventions has been built up within the EP profession.

The main questionnaire

The first set of questions was concerned with the way in which EPs made their initial assessments when presented by teachers with a new case (Table 3.1).

Table 3.1   The form of initial assessment of the problem

	Percentage answering yes
1 Was the problem described in behavioural (i.e. precise, observable) terms?	89
2 Was informal classroom observation carried out by the EP?	84
3 Were baseline measures taken by the teacher?	59
4 Were psychometric (norm-referenced) tests used by the EP?	29
5 Were baseline measures taken by the EP?	28
6 Were other forms of assessment used?	60

A wide range of 'other forms' of preliminary assessment was mentioned, by far the most common being the collection of information from, and the opinions of, parents. As many of these items were mentioned only once or twice, these responses are presented numerically in Table 3.2 rather than as percentages of the total sample.

Stating the problem in behavioural terms, a cornerstone of the behavioural approach, was not surprisingly a characteristic of 89 per cent of the programmes. In answer to the question about how long it took to arrive at this, a wide range of responses, from 5 minutes to 90 minutes, was obtained. These replies confirm that formulating a description of a child's behaviour in terms of actions which are observable, and avoiding inferential judge-

Table 3.2   Other forms of preliminary assessment

	Number of programmes
Meeting with parents	16
Discussion or interview with child	4
Brief reading assignment for the teacher	2
Assess child's academic abilities	2
Assess amount and quality of work produced by child	2
Discussion with parents and social worker	1
Discussion with previous teacher	1
Sociometry tasks for the teacher	1
Assess child's response to various reinforcers	1
Description from dinner supervisors/ non-teaching assessment	1
Description of strategies already used and outcomes	1
Observations in playground and at home	1

ments about either motives or personality characteristics, can be a time-consuming process during the initial discussions between an EP and a teacher.

On the other hand, these figures suggest that this is not always the case, implying that there are some teachers or some EPs who find observable descriptions easy to make, or that there are some children's problems that yield readily to them, and some which definitely do not.

In more than four out of five interventions, the EP sat in on the class to carry out some informal observation activities. In contrast, psychometric testing was employed on only 29 per cent of occasions. The use of behavioural approaches may thus be seen as bringing EPs far more into classrooms.

Similarly, in 29 per cent of interventions, EPs actually carried out baseline measurements in classrooms, although this task was performed by teachers themselves on 59 per cent of occasions. In total, baseline recording, another fundamental component of the behavioural approach, was undertaken by one party or both in 74 per cent of interventions.

In total, EPs spent a considerable amount of time – a mean of 2 hours and 14 minutes, and ranging between 25 minutes and 5½ hours – on these preliminary assessments before proceeding to the next phase, the development of an intervention plan.

Strategy planning

A major feature of the behavioural approach is the identification of one or more target behaviours to attempt to increase or decrease. In the programmes sampled, 85 per cent included the identification of a target behaviour to increase. Of those which did, there was almost unanimous agreement (87 per cent) to work on the child either remaining seated or completing set amounts of work – being 'on task'. The few remaining interventions were concerned with more specific problems such as being responsible for graffiti in the toilets or having difficulty in separating from a parent at the beginning of the school day.

Figure 3.1 The forms and delivery of reinforcers (from Miller, 1989a)

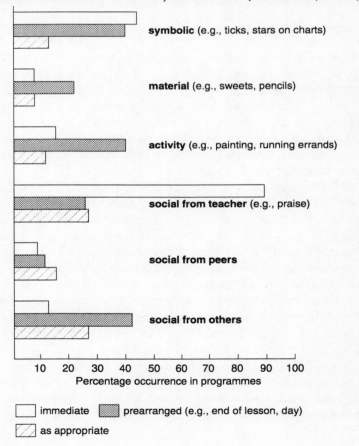

A target behaviour to decrease was chosen in 73 per cent of programmes. Specifically, a pupil leaving his seat was seen by 44 per cent as a behaviour to attempt to decrease. Calling or shouting out in class was the next most frequent, at 24 per cent. Figure 3.1 shows the types of reinforcement included in the programmes and the ways in which these were presented to the children. Fifty-five per cent of respondents indicated that they used 'other reinforcers'. The items they offered are listed here in Table 3.3.

Table 3.3   Other reinforcers

Home–school link
Parent record
Daily visit to valued neighbour
Home–school report system/pocket money
Parental praise
Achievement slip for parents
Errands
Sticker/certificate home
Response cost
Progress report to parents half-way through
Diary of good behaviour sent home
Parents to give extra TV time/social worker to give outings
Having hair done in plaits
Home/school book
House point
Leave school early on Friday/pocket money from parents
Small presents
Parent allows child to select a video to watch
Parent and child decide rewards on basis of daily diary home from school
Pudding
Weekly visit to clinic for computer games
Colouring section of a large picture
Trip to park with parents
Letter sent home
Certificate to take home to parents/daily diary from teacher and child
    compared
Playing the piano
Sheltered play with chosen others
Chart/certificate home
Tidying art cupboard/choosing a friend to sharpen pencils with
Sticker from headteacher
Pocket money

In 16 of these programmes, more than half of the list, a link between home and school was established. In many ways these programmes could have been categorized within Figure 3.1 except that the reinforcers were, in the main, delivered out of school. Table 3.3 can be collapsed in the following way:

	(No. of cases)
Symbolic	2
Material	6
Activity	12
Social from teacher	15
Social from peers	0
Social from others	19

This list assumes that teacher–parent communication schemes involved social praise from both teachers and parents, and shows a similar trend to the pattern of reinforcers used in school.

Returning to these, Table 3.4 looks more closely at those reinforcers said to be given at a pre-arranged time and shows, for the category of reinforcer, the percentage of programmes that involved reward delivery within the lesson, at the end of the lesson, at the end of the half day, at the end of the day and at the end of the week.

Table 3.4   Categories of reinforcers delivered at different pre-arranged times

Reinforcer	Within lesson	End of lesson	End of half-day	End of day	End of week
Symbolic (N=20)	10	50	20	5	15
Material (N=11)	—	9	9	36	45
Activity (N=19)	5	16	16	21	42
Social from teacher (N=14)	7	36	21	21	14
Social from peers (N=0)	—	—	—	—	—
Social from others (N=17)	—	—	18	47	35

Table 3.4 shows a high proportion of the symbolic reinforcers being given at the end of lessons rather than at other times. This accords with what seems least intrusive but not too distant in time for the link to have become too weakened. Again, perhaps to avoid intrusion, more time-consuming and 'larger' categories such as activities and material reinforcers are given far more frequently at the end of the week. In between these, the category of 'social from others' – possibly parents involved in home–school links – occurred most frequently at the end of the day but also at a high rate at the end of the week.

The most prominent features of Figure 3.1 and Tables 3.3 to 3.6 are the very high incidence of immediate social reinforcement from the teachers and the ignoring of undesired behaviour, the high usage of symbolic reinforcers both immediately and at more convenient times, usually the end of lessons, and the provision of favoured activities at pre-arranged times. The low incidence of material rewards at any time counters any charges that EPs and teachers are involved in such programmes in at least the cruder forms of 'bribery'.

Table 3.5   Use of sanctions

Sanction	Percentage of programmes
Ignoring	72
Time out	39
Punishment	9

Table 3.6   Persons other than teachers or peers providing social reinforcement

	Percentage of programmes
Parents	40
Headteacher	24
EP	4
Non-teaching assistant	3
Grandparent	3
Another teacher	3
Dinner supervisor	3
Sibling	1

The frequent involvement of parents as additional agents of approval and encouragement may be seen either as merely an extra-potent reinforcer or as a means by which more harmonious relationships between home and school can be encouraged. The very low figures for punishment should also help dispel some persistent misconceptions that behavioural approaches involve the use of threatening and punishing activities.

Even after devoting, in many cases, a number of hours to the assessment of factors involved in a pupil's difficult behaviour, a workable intervention strategy may not readily be forthcoming. For example, 29 per cent of EPs stated that there had been difficulties in agreeing upon a strategy with the class teacher.

Altering aspects of the classroom environment

A behavioural strategy may have more success if certain setting conditions or antecedents such as aspects of the classroom organization or the curriculum are changed. A section of the questionnaire examined these issues and the replies are summarized in Table 3.7.

Table 3.7   Alterations made to classroom organization as part of the strategy

	Percentage of programmes
Child's seating changed	51
Amount of work for child increased	43
Classroom rules explained differently	42
Distractions removed from child	40
Work for child changed	32
Amount of work for child reduced	17
Other changes	16
Classroom rules changed for child	12
Classroom rules changed for whole class	5
At least one aspect of classroom organization changed	85

This table shows, among other things, that changes are made to at least one aspect of classroom organization in a large majority of the interventions. The most prominent of these aspects is moving a child's seating position, which occurs in one out of every two programmes. It also shows that many of the items that may be viewed as more 'permissive', such as reducing the child's workload or making exceptions from the class rules, are much less frequently employed. It may well be that these 'allowances' would be likely to arouse teachers' reservations about unfairness and are thus avoided for this reason. On the other hand, incorporating into a programme the expectations that a child will achieve greater amounts of work clearly helps create a positive climate.

It is tempting to ask why these classroom changes, fairly ordinary routine matters in many ways, are necessary. Why has the teacher not tried them before? Does the behavioural programme in fact serve in some way as an elaborate Trojan Horse within which some very simple management procedures, which may have been overlooked in the face of the presenting problem, can be introduced into the classroom? The discussion a little later in this chapter of 'elements of programmes affecting outcomes' suggests that there may be some truth in this suggestion.

Monitoring of the evaluation

Table 3.8 shows how the intervention was monitored and the extent to which various changes were made during implementation. Figure 3.2 then indicates the number of visits in total made by the EP during implementation and Figure 3.3 shows how long after initiating the intervention the first of these visits occurred.

Table 3.8   Monitoring of the intervention

	Interventions (%)
Criteria for ending programme set in advance	41
Measures taken during implementation	63
Visits made during implementation	85
Changes made during implementation to:	
– target behaviour(s)	34
– reinforcer(s)	24
– punishment(s)	6
– setting events (i.e. classroom environment)	25
– any other changes	26
Decision made before starting about:	
– a review date	75
– an ending date	21
Intervention longer than originally expected	50
Intervention shorter than originally expected	50

Figure 3.2   The number of visits made by the EP during the implementation of the strategy (*N*=38)

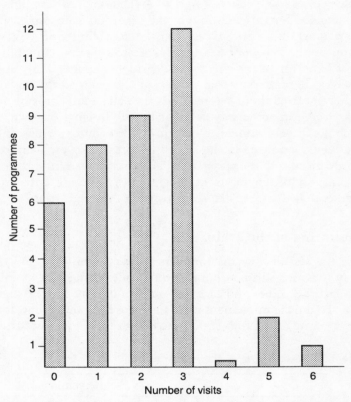

Of the 38 replies to the question about the number of visits, 84 per cent made at least one visit, 32 per cent achieved the modal value of three visits and only 8 per cent carried out more than this.

Figure 3.3 shows that four weeks was the most favoured interval before the first review (in 30 per cent of instances), with only 32 per cent taking longer than this.

Table 3.9 indicates that the teacher is very much in charge of most changes made during the programme, although alterations to the target behaviour were as likely to be a joint decision between the teacher and EP. The major sole responsibility of the EP was for any changes to the reinforcers, whereas by far the biggest shared responsibility was the decision to discontinue the intervention. This information dispels any notion that strategies

Figure 3.3   Period within which the first review date was set (N = 50)

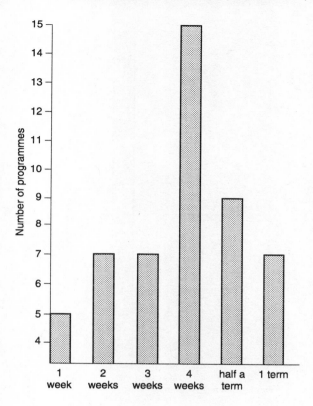

are somehow imposed upon teachers, or at least that teachers are following some course of action which does not command their support for any length of time.

Table 3.9   Person initiating changes during implementation (percentage of programmes)

Changes to	Teacher	EP	Joint
Target behaviour	48	9	43
Reinforcer	50	25	25
Setting conditions	75	16	8
Other changes	68	16	16
Discontinuing	31	3	66

Figure 3.4   Eventual length of the intervention (*N*=60)

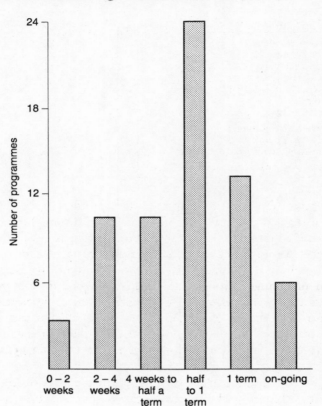

Figure 3.4 shows that the majority of interventions (40 per cent) lasted between half a term and a full term, with only 20 per cent being discontinued within a month or less. A further 32 per cent were longer than one term in duration.

Methods of evaluation

Some form of evaluation always takes place during any educational intervention. It may be only at the level of opinions and impressions of various participants and observers, or it may be in the form of more rigorous quantitative measures. Table 3.10 shows the means of evaluation employed in the 68 programmes under study.

Table 3.10   Means of evaluation employed

Means of evaluation employed	Percentage of programmes
Class teacher satisfaction	90
Parent satisfaction	35
Headteacher satisfaction	31
Child satisfaction	13
Other teacher's satisfaction	6
Grandparent's satisfaction	3
Welfare assistant's satisfaction	1
Class teacher written report	35
Repeat of baseline measures	29
Repeat of other preliminary measures	26
Satisfaction, without accompanying written evaluation	42

The ways in which programmes are actually evaluated, as shown in Table 3.10, raise a fundamental issue. The number of programmes that included a baseline measurement at the end of the intervention fell to 29 per cent, from an initial level of 74 per cent. Behavioural psychologists consider the objective demonstration of change through the comparison of pre- and post-intervention measurements of target behaviour to be essential. Schweiso (1985), for example, states quite clearly that 'the demonstration of the effectiveness of an intervention is an integral part of the behavioural approach rather than an optional extra'.

The survey shows a clear preference on the part of EPs for leaving evaluation at the level of expressed satisfaction of the class teacher and, in about one-third of programmes, of the head teacher and parent as well.

Why should this be so? One likely explanation is that part of the negotiated agreement between the EP and the teacher, probably implicit, was that the teacher would be involved in the minimum of additional duties over and above the usual classroom routines. Schweiso acknowledges that busy practitioners will be more interested in what happens as a result of an intervention rather than in being able to demonstrate exactly how it happened.

The problem for EPs is probably that they see themselves as busy practitioners as well as research-minded behavioural psychologists. Because of the need to adapt techniques to a set of constraints imposed by schools, EPs are likely to experience some degree of role strain and, because their interventions appear to 'fall short' of reported case studies, they may well be reluctant to publish and disseminate these 'less than complete' interventions.

A major aim of this study, of course, is to describe the actual widespread behaviour of professionals in applied settings, in the belief that this, in itself, is a body of data from which important lessons can be drawn.

However, if this explains why baseline measures are not usually repeated after an intervention, it then raises the question of why they are so frequently included before. One probable explanation is that they present a yardstick with which to compare data collected *during* the intervention, providing evidence of change and hence acting as a source of motivation. However, it is also possible that aspects of actually observing and recording an initial baseline serve to encourage the teacher to construe the child's behaviour in a different fashion. Harrop (1977), for instance, working with groups of teachers in workshop settings, regularly found that about one in six teachers reported improvements after the initial baseline period – before any attempt was made at implementing a strategy.

Outcomes of evaluation

What ultimately, then, are the outcomes of these evaluations? Table 3.11 shows the degrees of improvement judged to have taken place as percentages of the total number of programmes using that method of evaluation.

The results are generally very positive. The programmes in

Table 3.11 Outcomes of different forms of evaluation as perceived by EPs

Means of evaluation	Considerable improvement	Moderate improvement	No change
Class teacher satisfaction	38	52	8
Satisfaction of others	40	43	16
Class teacher's written reports	29	58	12
Repeat of baseline measures	35	45	20
Repeat of preliminary measures	17	61	22

which there was no change in the pupil's behaviour are relatively few, although it should be noted that this change is a little harder to demonstrate by a repeated baseline measure than by a class teacher's expression of satisfaction. Of course, how much improvement respondents classified as 'moderate' is not known, but even if only the 'considerable improvement' category is considered, these figures are encouraging when one bears in mind that the problems under consideration had all been deemed serious enough to warrant referral to an EP.

Most frequently occurring elements within programmes

One of the aims of this section of the study was to provide a description of the most common forms of behavioural interventions being negotiated between EPs and primary school teachers. Most of this information can be gleaned from Tables 3.1 to 3.11 but Table 3.12 provides a summary of all those elements and activities that were found to occur in more than half of the programmes.

Elements of programmes affecting outcomes

The study shows that certain elements figure very frequently in the behavioural interventions devised by EPs and primary school teachers for pupils displaying disruptive classroom behaviour. It also shows that certain practical, theoretical, ethical and inter-actional aspects are commonplace in the discussions during the setting up and implementation of these programmes. Interestingly, it shows that other practicalities and issues are not as frequently encountered as might be expected.

But of all the various elements and procedures examined, are some more essential for successful outcomes than others? Some may be necessary to gain teachers' participation in the first place, some may be included because of their traditional appearance in the literature, but do they all make an equal contribution towards a programme's effectiveness?

To answer this question, the presence or absence of each item on the questionnaire was considered in terms of whether it was associated for each programme with considerable improvement

Table 3.12   Most frequently occurring elements of programmes (those occurring in more than 50 per cent of the programmes)

	Percentage of programmes
Initial assessment	
Informal classroom observation by EP	84
Problem stated in behavioural terms	89
Baseline measures by teacher	59
Other initial measures	60
Strategy planning	
Target behaviour to increase chosen	85
Target behaviour to decrease chosen	73
Child involved in strategy planning	53
Reinforcement	
Immediate social reinforcement from teacher	87
Use of ignoring	72
Teachers' reservations	
Classroom practicalities	61
EPs' attempts to overcome teachers' reservations	
By describing examples from previous experience	81
By other means	54
Alterations to classroom organization	
Child's seating position changed	51
Management of strategy	
Measures taken during implementation	63
Visits made during implementation	85
Review date set in advance	75
End initiated by teacher and EP jointly	61
Methods of evaluation	
Class teacher's satisfaction	90
Satisfaction of others (all)	63
Factors restricting effectiveness	
EP's time	59

or not, as judged by the class teacher – this being the major evaluation method used and hence also yielding the most data. Of all the elements discussed in the tables in this section, only three were differentially represented in the two outcome categories at a statistically significant level.

Table 3.13   Factors associated with differential outcomes as judged by teacher satisfaction (percentage of programmes)

	Considerable improvement	Moderate improvement or no change
Classroom rules explained differently	59	32
Difficulties in agreeing strategies with teachers	8	43
Other changes made during the strategy (i.e. other than changes to target behaviours and reinforcers)	9	32

The third item in Table 3.13, 'other changes made during the strategy', does not refer to any one specific alteration and is thus difficult to interpret. Table 3.9 shows that in 68 per cent of instances these 'other changes' are initiated by the teacher, with only 16 per cent originating solely with the EP and another 16 per cent jointly. In other words, when changes are made in the strategy other than to target behaviours, reinforcers, or setting conditions, and these changes are most likely to be made by the teachers acting independently, then these changes are connected with the failure of the intervention. As these are changes made after implementation has begun, they may therefore be a consequence of a strategy that has seemed to the teacher to be failing, rather than a cause of a strategy that fails.

The 'difficulties in agreeing strategies with teachers' item suggests that programmes which are put into effect in such circumstances are significantly more likely to fail. This certainly suggests that more attention to the whole issue of teachers' reservations may be necessary in some cases and also casts doubts upon whether encouraging an experimental attitude is always a useful strategy if some prior disagreement has been encountered. One practical outcome from this may be that during consultation

EPs may be able to make explicit the research finding that unless difficulties in reaching some basic agreement are resolved, then the outcome of an intervention is unlikely to be particularly favourable.

The first item in Table 3.13 is the only one to be associated with increasing positive outcomes. It is reassuring to see that explaining classroom rules differently during a strategy (it may be that they had not been specifically articulated before) is the particular item, as this was one of the three factors involved in the original Madsen *et al.* study (1968).

Of course the item 'classroom rules explained differently' does not in itself indicate which rules these were, nor the manner in which they were subsequently presented. However, it is possible to gain at least an impression of these changes from the added and unsolicited comments that respondents made about this item on their questionnaires, and these verbatim comments are shown in Table 3.14.

Table 3.14   Further details of classroom rules being explained differently, as provided by nine respondents

Made explicit as part of the programme
Discussion with child about wandering around the class
Made more specific
Not differently, just more closely stuck to
During time out
To the child for clarification
Rules about sitting and completing tasks and what to do then simply
    made more explicit
More detailed description of what was required
Simplified, personal and direct

The common themes in this list seem to be the clarification and simplifying of classroom rules, probably being explained to the particular pupil individually and then being adhered to more consistently by the teacher. This is somewhat inferential and only based on nine replies, but the comments seem consistent with each other and have at least a surface plausibility. One can imagine that an EP who only recommended this course of action would be treated with some scepticism and there are thus grounds for viewing the overall programme as a means of introducing this seemingly potent ingredient. Of course, this is not to suggest that all other elements are unimportant. Many may appear quite different in practice when implemented by teachers and EPs, and may interact with each other or have a cumulative effect. But the study does endorse strongly the inclusion of a restatement of rules in any programme, the one of the three original independent variables of Madsen *et al.* which this study has revealed to feature less prominently in behavioural interventions.

Factors perceived as restricting an intervention's effectiveness

Table 3.15 shows that time constraints, for the EP even more than the teacher, are perceived as the major impediment to strategies being more successful. Items relating to co-operation on the part of school personnel figure much less highly – class teacher co-operation, which is the highest of these items, being seen to restrict the effectiveness in less than one-third of programmes.

Table 3.15 Factors perceived as restricting an intervention's effectiveness

	Percentage of interventions
Time EP could allocate to intervention	59
Time teacher could allocate to intervention	45
Other factors	39
Teacher's understanding of approach	38
Type of presenting problems	30
Child's co-operation	29
EP's knowledge and experience	29
Teacher's co-operation	23
Headteacher's understanding	21
Headteacher's co-operation	12
Other staff in the school	10

THE LIMITED TAKE-UP OF BEHAVIOURAL APPROACHES

Despite all this discussion in the literature, the accumulation of replicated research studies and the methodical accounts of practitioners' consultative endeavours, despite the attention paid both to theoretical developments and to the practical issues involved in implementing interventions in classrooms, it remains the case that behavioural approaches have made only limited inroads into the educational scene.

Dessent (1988) has argued that, despite the high degree of interest in behavioural methods shown by the EP profession in Britain, there has been low take-up and maintenance of the resulting techniques over time in schools. He attributes this phenomenon to the possibility that behavioural approaches may make unrealistic demands on resources, in terms of teachers' time, effort and classroom reorganization. He asks whether some of these approaches are 'compatible with the realities of busy classroom life' and suggests that attention could be profitably switched from 'ever more fine-grained task analysis' to helping develop actual teaching resources. He also suggests that if EPs wish behavioural approaches to find more favour with teachers, they should stop trying to present them as discoveries from within psychology and focus on 'the behavioural principles which are evident in good teaching'.

This same lack of take-up has also been reported in North America, where Axelrod *et al.* (1990) have suggested that factors from outside have obstructed the 'dissemination of behavioural technology' and 'characteristics of the behavioural approach ... have diminished its use'. In terms of factors outside the techniques, these writers identify what they see as the pervasive influence of psychodynamic approaches, the negative image of behavioural approaches as being associated with control, and its off-putting terminology. From within the approach itself, they draw attention to the fact that research appears to be too concentrated upon 'what we already know a lot about and too little on what we do not. Areas that we know too little about are treatment adherence ... – how to get people to do it right, and treatment acceptance ... – how to get people to do it at all'.

In view of this repeated pattern of the demonstrated useful-
ness and effectiveness of behavioural approaches and the
continuing reservations of many within schools towards them,
it is time to address this professional reluctance. Consequently,
the next chapter examines directly what is known about the
reactions and reservations of teachers in respect of behavioural
approaches.

CHAPTER 4

The reactions and reservations of teachers

From the very beginning, teachers have frequently expressed reservations about behavioural approaches. Thus, in the first demonstration of the successful use of a behavioural intervention in a British school, Ward (1971) concluded that 'the communication of advice may be the most demanding part of the programme'. This chapter will review what experienced educational psychologists who have been significant proponents of these approaches have had to say about teachers' reactions and reservations, as well as look at the relatively small body of research evidence about this particular subject.

THE VIEWS OF EARLY PROPONENTS OF BEHAVIOURAL APPROACHES

In many of the papers written by Presland in the early and mid 1970s, which served to extend the base of successful behavioural casework in mainstream and special education settings, a concern with gaining the interest and enthusiastic support of teachers is apparent (Presland, 1972, 1973a, 1973b, 1974). By 1975, he was able to offer an extended discussion of what he termed the 'practical problems' of advising schools on the use of behavioural approaches. These included the realization that attempting to encourage the take-up of these approaches by such means as an introductory pamphlet was seldom successful because teachers seemed to require 'specific answers for a particular child'.

He also found it difficult to deliver a programme to the staff of a secondary school because of the reliance this placed upon the skills and understanding of the school's 'contact person'. Meeting the charge from teachers that 'we've tried all that', Presland contended that closer examination usually revealed that either the stage of obtaining a precise definition of the problem behaviour had been omitted, or teacher attention towards a pupil intended to be punishing was in fact acting as a positive reinforcer, or there was a lack of consistency in the application of the technique. Presland (1975) also suggested that, in some instances, teachers might want the pupil removed from the school rather than retained by means of an intervention strategy, or that they may hold firmly a 'medical model' of deviant behaviour, or have reservations on ethical grounds about the apparent element of bribery within the approach. To counter all these reservations, he recommended that practitioners equip themselves with *accounts of successful practice* to relay to teachers (Presland, 1975).

After conducting the very first British case study, Ward continued to experiment with the approach and, in 1976, was able to condense his thoughts about teachers' fears and reservations and the ways in which these might be allayed. Where Presland had referred to 'practical problems', Ward used the term 'implementation issues' to refer to the whole area of the relationship and interactions between the EP as consultant and the teachers who are seeking help and advice. (In this book, these topics will usually be subsumed under the term 'consultation'.) Ward warned that school staff would be resistant to the changes proposed by a consultant offering behavioural approaches unless a number of conditions were met:

- staff felt ownership of the strategy;
- there was wholehearted support from all involved;
- the strategy accorded with existing values;
- the participants' autonomy and security were not threatened;

- the participants felt the change would reduce their burdens, rather than increase them as in some detailed and demanding ('heavy') interventions;
- the participants contributed to the planning, which was difficult to achieve in large schools;
- there was trust and confidence amongst all concerned ('a feature of BM programmes is the remorseless identification of weak teaching');
- attitudes were open-minded, allowing for reconsideration and revision if necessary.

Finally, on the issue of conclusions drawn by practitioners from their extensive casework experience, Winter (1983a, 1983b) proposed a set of recommended actions (68 in all!) for EPs working with teachers' specific reservations. These papers represented a major synthesis, written obviously from the perspective of an advocate for behavioural methods and in the style of a set of 'tips' for psychologists. For example, he recommended that an EP should always actually see a child, 'however unnecessary it may appear', so that a sceptical teacher or parent would know that, as a consultant, 'you know what you are talking about'.

SYSTEMATIC STUDIES OF TEACHERS' RESERVATIONS

There are a number of reasons why teachers may have expressed reservations about behavioural approaches. There is the possibility that they lack an initial plausibility – 'face validity' – or that they do not easily accord with the way teachers typically operate within a classroom, or that the approach has little to offer in the areas of most concern to teachers.

In terms of the *initial plausibility* of behavioural approaches, Wheldall and Congreave (1980) carried out an anonymous survey of 116 mature students who were following advanced courses in education, in order to assess their attitudes towards 'behaviour modification' and its use in educational settings. The group's overall mean score suggested a general ambivalence of attitude, the sample as a whole being neither strongly opposed to, nor in favour of, the approach. Neither sex, age, number of years of teaching experience nor the age of children taught were significantly related to attitude score, but there was evidence to suggest a strong positive relationship between attitude score and prior knowledge of behaviour modification by study or practical experience.

Wheldall and Congreave then retested 44 of this original sample after they had completed a course in behavioural approaches and found significantly more positive attitude scores. This study demonstrates that the more teachers know about behavioural approaches, the more positive they are likely to be towards them. It should however be pointed out that a positive attitude does not imply that implementation will automatically or even easily follow.

If plausibility or acceptability increase with familiarization, do behavioural approaches initially *fit easily alongside the typical classroom behaviour of teachers*? It might be the case that they are directly antipathetic to some teachers' preferred or natural styles or that they are so similar as to lead to a lack of interest on the part of teachers because they feel that *nothing new is being offered* to them.

Some clarification of this issue is offered in a study by Merrett and Wheldall (1987) in which 128 teachers were observed in their classrooms. Using a specially constructed instrument, OPTIC, the rates at which teachers offered approval and disapproval were recorded and, in general, more approval than disapproval was observed. However, although there was a high rate of approval for academic behaviour, it was found that pupils were rarely commended for appropriate conduct but frequently reprimanded when it was inappropriate.

This finding suggests that the very frequently recommended use of teacher praise as a reinforcer in behavioural strategies may conflict with more naturally occurring teacher styles. Where teachers are not conscious of this aspect of their own behaviour, where there may be the greatest need for a positive intervention, there could be a strong tendency for them to assume that recommendations that include approval directed at appropriate conduct are stating the obvious, thus devaluing the credibility of the advice and, probably, its proponent.

This study suggests that pupils in certain teachers' classrooms might benefit significantly from some typically prominent aspects of behavioural interventions. A further study by Wheldall and Merrett (1988), replicated for the Elton Committee, found that such interventions would also be particularly *appropriate for the types of classroom difficulties most troublesome to teachers.* Wheldall and Merrett (1988) sent out a questionnaire to a 25 per cent random sample of all infant, junior and infant–junior schools in a West Midlands LEA and received a reply rate of 93 per cent. Of the 198 teachers from 32 schools who replied, 51 per cent believed they were spending more time than they ought on problems of control and order. The most troubling type of behaviour, mentioned on 47 per cent of returns, could be subsumed under the heading of 'talking out of turn' and the next most troubling, occurring in 25 per cent of the sample, was 'hindering other children'.

These are very much the types of difficulties for which the accumulating body of research and practice suggests that a behavioural approach is particularly suited. Had the survey revealed, say, more intense forms of physical assault to be the most worrying for teachers of this age group, then classroom management procedures deriving from the behavioural literature would not necessarily have seemed so appropriate.

These systematically conducted studies should provide considerable encouragement to proponents of behavioural approaches. They demonstrate that teachers will become more positive towards them after a period of training in their rationale and practical aspects. And yet, practitioner EPs who work with teachers on a casework basis have continued to wrestle with the reluctance they have often found within schools towards recommendations based on a research literature which, to these EPs, has come to look increasingly compelling. As Leach (1981) put it,

> Why have behavioural models for assessment and intervention not yet been adopted as routine problem-solving and preventative strategies in schools, despite their ... convincing data-base?

To understand this phenomenon further, it is necessary to extend the discussion beyond the reactions of individual teachers and look at the organizational contexts in which these teachers work. There is a need to examine the possible effects that actually working in a school has upon the ways teachers make sense of difficult pupil behaviour and the plausibility of various approaches towards its improvement.

CASEWORK EXPERIENCE AND SCHOOL LEVEL FACTORS

In attempting to answer his own question about the very slow adoption rate for behavioural approaches within schools, Leach (1981) confesses that he had once thought the culprit was the 'clinical–pathological' perspective on children's behaviour. He saw it as having a general appeal to both psychologists and teachers. To the former it helped confer professional status as a result of using 'exclusive psychometric apparatus, secret diagnostic ritual, hypothetical constructs about unseen mental faculties, pseudo-medical diagnostic labels and deceptively precise statistical prediction'. For the teacher, whether or not the psychologist's 'findings' were accepted, there was a reassurance, Leach argued, in being given an explanation of a child's difficulties in terms of 'within-child' factors which thus absolved the teacher from any part in the original problem or its solution.

Leach went on to argue that he had changed his view and come to see the lack of take-up of behavioural approaches as being not solely the result of their potential for upsetting this mutually supportive style of practice, but also as being caused by psychologists' lack of attention to the whole issue of the practice of consultation:

> We have neglected to face the fact that we are dealing with slow-changing permanent systems (i.e. schools) ... We have, therefore, not considered the need for developing system-change skills as vital extras to basic intervention expertise.

These thoughts are echoed in the conclusions from the Teacher–Child Interaction Project where Berger *et al.* (1987), after collecting a considerable amount of data over an extended period, asserted that

> emphasis must also be placed on optimising conditions in such a way that teachers do use the skills. Such work would need to recognise the importance of the school as an organisation and the influence this has on the change potential of individual teachers.

67

And again, Gersch (1983), another experienced EP, emphasized that in working with teachers in this way, it was necessary to attend to aspects of the school system – 'its hierarchy, structure, and "hidden rules".'

It is not difficult to speculate upon the way in which various school-level processes may become implicated in individual teachers' reactions. For instance, the question often arises of a style of delivery or differentiation of the curriculum for a particular child or even the whole class, and it may be necessary to consider whether a child's disruptiveness is partly the result of boredom or repeated failure (McNamara, 1982). If this is a possibility, does the classroom organization permit a change of activities for one child? What should such activities consist of anyway? It may be that there are fixed class or school policies on curriculum or procedures which appear to give a clear benefit to the majority of pupils and cannot be changed because such changes would be seen as the 'thin end of the wedge', leading inevitably to the dismantling of successful practice. The survey evidence reported in Chapter 3, for instance, shows that a promising solution might involve some physical movement for the child to a new seating position. The physical structure of the classroom or the whole school, or the use that is made of it by other staff, may prevent this.

Similarly, a strategy might benefit from the involvement of other members of staff and there may be questions over the likelihood of this co-operation (Ward, 1976). If the reported behaviour problem has led to some degree of acrimony between the child's parents and the school and a prerequisite for a solution appears to be a reconciliation of viewpoints and purposes, will there be a willingness on the part of all involved to work towards this? If there is not, and the EP is still expected to resolve the problem because this is a role expectation or obligation, should she or he first attempt to bring together the opposing parties?

Practitioners also find that teachers are sometimes reluctant to be involved in programmes that seem to include aspects of 'bribery', 'disproportionate attention to one child', or 'rewarding naughty children' (Presland, 1975, 1978). When these concerns cannot be dispelled by talking through the issues, how feasible is it to consider a change of teacher? Given the implied criticism or attributions of inadequacy which surround changing a child's teacher, headteachers are likely to be extremely reluctant to condone such a course of action and teacher colleagues to accept it. These school-level factors may well have an influence on the eventual form or even acceptability of any intervention, over and above any considerations of an individual teacher's attitudes and opinions.

THE EP SURVEY AND TEACHERS' RESERVATIONS

The questionnaire survey of EPs described in Chapter 3 also presented an opportunity to investigate further some of the details of teachers' initial reactions to recommended behavioural interventions and the ensuing planning discussions. Replies to a question concerning this first aspect are shown in Table 4.1.

Table 4.1   Teachers' initial reservations about strategy

Did the teacher appear to have initial reservations about	Percentage 'Yes'
Practical problems of implementation?	61
Fairness (rewarding only one child)?	46
Issues of bribery?	27
Praise not being spontaneous?	16
Other matters?	34

A variety of other matters was raised by teachers at this stage of strategy planning, the most common being a rather generally stated disbelief in the strategy working. Because of the relatively small number of cases for each item, these frequencies are presented in Table 4.2 in absolute terms rather than as percentages.

Clearly, in the light of such a range of reservations, and in instances of serious disagreement over the strategy, a number of demands will be made upon EPs' skills. The plan may either need to be amended, perhaps even abandoned, or the teachers may need to be helped to overcome their reservations. A question in the survey asked EPs about their responses to these reservations and the replies are shown in Table 4.3.

Table 4.2   Other reservations

	Number of programmes
Disbelief in likely effectiveness	6
Intervention too 'simple' for massiveness of problem	3
Teacher's concern about his or her own ability to behave consistently	2
Amount of time required	2
Child might become bored with the programme if it went on for too long	1
Child might become dependent on rewards	1
Difficulties getting support from home	1
Would changes generalize beyond the half-hour per day of the programme?	1
Possible lack of motivation on the part of other teachers	1
Problem seen as in child's character	1
Programme not seen as part of duties	1
Teacher did not see problem as major but headteacher did	1

Table 4.3   EPs' responses to teachers' reservations

If teacher had reservations, how did you attempt to overcome them?	Percentage 'Yes'
By describing similar examples from your previous experience	81
By lending or recommending a book or article	26
By asking the teacher to trust your judgement	19
By describing examples from the literature	17
By leaving a handout prepared by yourself	11
By other means	54

Table 4.4 expands verbatim the responses made in the 'other means' category.

Tables 4.2, 4.3 and 4.4 reveal a complex pattern of issues likely to lead to discussion, negotiation, modification or rejection of the strategy. Clearly, teachers present problems of fitting the strategy into their ordinary classroom routine as a major reservation rather than more 'ethical' issues, although these, as well as a belief in 'within-child' origins of problems and a doubt in their own abilities, were also mentioned.

In response, EPs appear to take an approach that is far more

Table 4.4 Other means of attempting to overcome reservations

	Number of programmes
Short story to put teacher in the place of child (emotional insight)	1
Recommending other teacher to talk to	2
Discussion of behavioural principles and modifying programme to fit teacher's preferred working method	1
Talking through and listening to teacher's problems	1
Urging teacher to take an experimental view	1
Further investigation, seeking parent's view	1
Comparing with real-life issues, such as going to work for a salary	1
Observation of the process in action	1
Suggesting 'let's try it for 2 weeks and see'	3
Using an 'outcome justifying the means' argument	1
Refer to how reward systems work on us as adults all the time and how we are unconsciously rewarding all other children	1
Group discussion with other children	3
Discussion with a teacher who had been successful with such a programme	1
'Bribing' with more visits	1
Acknowledging teacher's feelings but negotiating input	1
'If you want my advice you will give it a fair trial'	1
Asking her to use her own judgement to fit the programme into her own routine	1
General discussion	1
Explaining that if child is sufficiently badly behaved, other children will understand 'different' treatment	1
Discussion, with written feedback of discussion	1
Regular 'topping up' meeting by EP and trainee EP	1
Encouraging a positive attitude, for an experimental period, and promising to return to monitor in an agreed time	1
Headteacher accepting child and encouraging teacher to review doubts as to level of professional ability	1
General discussion of her teaching strategies – 'she's already doing it'.	1

pragmatic than erudite, relaying examples from their previous experience, encouraging and providing support during an experimental period, and taking a role in creating supportive peer interactions for teachers. EPs also saw themselves as encouraging an experimental approach, sometimes by setting an early review date, within a week or two, when the EP would return and the programme would be changed or abandoned if it was proving unworkable or unsuccessful. A tendency not to over-prescribe the detail of a programme was also revealed and in some cases EPs gave a number of general suggestions and recognized that it was the teacher's professional contribution to adapt the programme and the usual classroom routine to each other. In still other instances, the support of professional colleagues was enlisted by introducing the teacher to another who had achieved positive outcomes in a similar situation, or by the EP gathering together a group of teachers in a school to create a joint responsibility for planning and implementing a strategy.

All these items display a range of consultative skills and it is hard to believe that the form of the strategy finally implemented is not being negotiated and modified during these conversations.

These survey results can be compared to the published accounts of practitioners described at the beginning of this chapter. It is interesting, for instance, to see from Table 4.3 that EPs who encounter reservations on the part of teachers attempt to meet these in a very high 81 per cent of instances with examples of success in their previous practice. Lending books or articles, or recourse to details from the research literature, figure considerably less prominently.

These results accord very closely with Presland's (1975) recommendation that practitioners equip themselves with accounts of successful practice when consulting with teachers who might feel some scepticism. Presland indicated that teachers might have reservations about interventions that appear to contain elements of 'bribery' or 'disproportionate attention to one child' and the survey suggests that these feelings remain, Table 4.1 indicating that they occur in 27 per cent and 46 per cent of interventions respectively. However, it is concern about practical problems such as the time available to implement a strategy that is voiced most frequently – on 61 per cent of occasions.

THE LIMITATIONS OF THE QUESTIONNAIRE SURVEY

Any claims that the study as reported so far can represent the final word on behavioural approaches in consultative contexts must be quickly tempered by considerations of the validity of the data. Although there are grounds for being reasonably optimistic about validity, it must, however, be remembered that this method of investigation relied completely on the reports of EPs. It did not directly approach the teachers themselves for their views and opinions or their accounts of what they actually did, said and felt, and this might have provided at the least a different slant of emphasis.

The evidence that has been reported in these opening chapters has indicated that behavioural approaches have a proven effectiveness. The evolution of practice has been characterized by a move away from 'behavioural overkill', with its heavy emphasis on rewards and punishments, and from the control and compliance implicit in too great a concern with 'on-task' behaviour, towards greater pupil autonomy and teacher reflectiveness.

From within their classes and schools, teachers have been able to temper any unrealistic suggestions by reminding outside personnel of the constraints upon a teacher's time and resources whilst fulfilling a demanding professional role. The evidence suggests that EPs have listened to these reservations and attempted to reach workable compromises between the demands of theory and the practicalities of classrooms. They are not engaged in a 'mindless technology' (Berger, 1979).

And yet, despite all of this, what is it that prevents these strategies, which could be helpful and seem so ideally tailored to the requirements of the Code of Practice, from gaining a far greater acceptability within schools?

To answer this question, and to move beyond the limitations of survey information from EPs, the next phase of this study now turns directly towards those professionals who have the major and immediate responsibility for managing difficult pupil behaviour – the recipients of these behavioural interventions, the classroom teachers. What do they really think and feel about all these recommendations?

PART 2

WORKING WITH TEACHERS AND TEACHER CULTURES

CHAPTER 5

The significance of teacher culture

RATIONALE FOR THE TEACHER INTERVIEW STUDY

This chapter, the rest of Part 2 and the whole of Part 3 are all constructed around the results obtained from an in-depth interview study with a sample of teachers. Previous chapters have shown that behavioural interventions have failed to gain widespread acceptance in schools, despite a convincing evidence base. As almost all the published accounts have been written by advocates of these approaches, the major part of this book turns to the viewpoints of teachers involved in these strategies in order to see whether such a perspective is able to cast new light on this pervasive and continuing phenomenon.

Ideally, an investigation attempting to understand the ways in which an EP and a teacher together plan a strategy and its subsequent implementation would be conducted in the form of observations of each stage of the process. This would probably be backed up by interviews with the major participants and perhaps enhanced by a range of 'objective' measures. However, this would impose a very complex and protracted schedule upon the collection of data. In the actual study of teachers described in this chapter, the sample was obtained from a geographical area whose extremities were two hundred miles apart. Tracking interventions across this distance and being present for the significant steps in each would have been logistically impossible.

Consequently, it was decided to focus upon teachers who had been the recipients of recommended strategies that had proved at least partially successful. It was hypothesized that had the sample also included teachers with unsuccessful strategies, these teachers might have been much more inclined to attribute such failures to causes external to themselves and hence the study might have been restricted in its explanatory potential. It was felt that interviewees would be much more amenable to detailed questioning and probing if this was directed towards a subject unlikely to provoke a sense of defensiveness.

IDENTIFICATION OF THE SAMPLE

Twenty-four primary teachers were interviewed using a structured interview. They were identified by contacting EPs in a number of local education authorities (LEAs) and asking whether they could supply the name and address of any primary range teacher with whom they had devised an intervention deriving to a greater or lesser degree from a behavioural perspective. The pupil's behaviour had to be of an unsettled or anti-social nature and the intervention needed to have been judged by the teacher within the last two months as having been at least partially successful.

THE INTERVIEW

The interviewing style was such as to encourage teachers to reflect and expand upon the points they made and interviews were conducted in undisturbed settings after school such as classrooms, the teachers' homes and the researcher's office and were between 40 minutes and an hour in duration. In the main, the prepared interview comprised open rather than closed questions in order to elicit the maximum amount of data. The interviewing style incorporated the specific behaviours identified by Cannel and Kahn (1968) as being likely to 'create and maintain an atmosphere in which the respondent feels that he is fully understood and in which it is safe to communicate fully without fear of being judged, criticized or subsequently identified and disadvantaged'.

The interviewer behaviours shown to facilitate this consist of: brief expressions of understanding and interest, brief expectant pauses, neutral requests for additional information, echo or near repetition of interviewee's words, summarizing or reflecting, requests for specific kinds of additional information, and repetition of a primary question. In addition to creating a particular atmosphere, Cannel and Kahn also suggest that such a style focuses attention on the content of the communication, encouraging the respondent to consider each topic as deeply, fully and frankly as the interview objectives require.

THE SAMPLE

The teachers

The 24 teachers identified were drawn from 8 LEAs spanning an area between the Midlands and the Scottish border. They were nominated for the study by 20 different EPs (2 EPs nominated 3 teachers each) and all but 2 taught in different schools. They had been working with primary age children for a mean of 11.6 years, the range being from 2 to 25 years.

The schools

The schools in which these teachers worked ranged in size from 71 to 484 pupils (excluding any nursery places), with a mean of 218.

The percentage of the school population eligible for free school meals in these schools was between 3 and 67, with a mean of 21 per cent.

National figures for a similar period (DES, 1991) indicated average primary school sizes of 193 pupils and a take-up rate for free school meals of 13 per cent, suggesting that the schools in the sample were not untypical of the average in terms of pupil numbers but were probably slightly higher in terms of social disadvantage.

All the teachers interviewed except one were women, whereas they were identified by 13 female and 7 male EPs. The sample included one teaching head, one deputy and three special needs co-ordinators.

The pupils

The pupils were drawn from the full primary age range with a bias towards the younger group, the mean age being 7.1 years. Of the 24 children only one was a girl.

In terms of the perceived severity of the problem behaviour the majority of the 24 teachers gave vivid accounts of the type frequently found in popular discussions of discipline and behaviour in schools:

> I've been teaching twelve years and I've never met such destructive, such wanton – under tables – attacking other children under tables. (Boy aged 5; Interview 1)

> Aggressive and disruptive and he didn't co-operate in a group, antisocial with his peers. (Boy aged 10; Teaching head, Interview 2)

> He's very destructive, very aggressive, spitting, bad language and so on ... I just felt well it's not doing them [the children] any good and it's not doing me any good and it's not doing my family any good. I came home at night and I was so wound up ... (Boy aged 6; Deputy head, Interview 3)

> Quite aggressive to teachers as well as children ... if you refused a request of his ... he'd be throwing chairs and leave the classroom, leave the school quite frequently as well. (Boy aged 10; Interview 22)

> A lot of physical abuse on teachers and people that were supporting him ... an incident of arson and various other things outside school. (Boy aged 6; Interview 23)

> He was causing a lot of problems for her [his mother] at home in that he was having tantrums, refusing to do whatever she told him, throwing things, swearing, kicking, generally uncontrollable for her. (Boy aged 5; Interview 24)

Ten teachers said the pupil was the most difficult they had ever encountered and eight said he or she was among the most difficult half-dozen.

GENERAL OUTCOMES OF THE INTERVENTIONS

The sample consisted of teachers who judged the behavioural interventions devised with the EP to have had positive outcomes. A selection of comments, again from the first three and last three interviews, as above, give a flavour of these responses:

> Quite honestly I can say I was knocked for six because it had worked and it has worked ever since. (Interview 1)

> I think it's now that he's found that it's easier for him if he co-operates in school. (Interview 2)

> I can honestly say he's not like the same child. (Interview 3)

> I think he was finally motivated to do something about it [behaviour] and it was quite evident he was very involved in this. (Interview 22)

> Towards the end of last term I felt very positive about what had been achieved ... but this term the last couple of weeks for some reason have been awful ... I'm hoping it was just Christmas ... and yesterday was a very good day. (Interview 23)

> It was one of those wonderful 'Ahh, this is great' – one of those wonderful success stories. (Interview 24)

In total, 6 interviewees expressed the view that the intervention had been successful but had some reservations, such as that there might be a deterioration again in the future (as in Interview 23); 11 saw a definite improvement with no qualifications (as in Interview 1); and 7 saw such a degree of success that it made a strong emotional impact on them (as in Interview 24).

THE NATURE OF GROUNDED THEORY METHODOLOGY

Grounded theory is a methodology developed by Glaser and Strauss (1967) which focuses upon theory generation rather than theory verification. It was developed within sociology out of a dissatisfaction with existing procedures which tended to generate large-scale theories that yielded little in the way of testable propositions. Glaser and Strauss believed that it would be more useful to develop 'middle range' or 'substantive' theories that explained a specific area of empirical enquiry. In their early writings, for example, they directed their attentions towards research that generated theories about various phenomena within medical practice, such as the nature and organization of work on a particular hospital ward and the management of pain (Strauss, 1987). Henwood and Pidgeon (1993) have argued that, although grounded theory is now being widely used in the 'human sciences', it has not yet made its mark to any great extent within the traditional areas of concern of the discipline of psychology.

The term 'grounded theory' has been criticized as misleading and Turner (1992) has suggested as an alternative the term 'developing local theory'. Turner argues that if the analysis is carried out thoroughly, generating substantive theory is likely to result in local variations of larger sociological or psychological theories rather than provide classic examples of them. It is Glaser and Strauss's contention that these larger-scale theories often do not offer a deep understanding of a range of phenomena but rather deny the complexity in data by forcing the data to fit within already established patterns of constructs. They believe that local theory should be grounded in the complexity of the data and that from local theories will emerge more all-embracing systems of understanding.

A quality grounded theory is one in which the researcher has been able to discover a core variable (Glaser, 1978). The process of analysis, which combines constant reference to the data with rigorous analytical thinking, will, it is claimed, eventually yield such a variable. Glaser defines the core variable as having three essential characteristics: it recurs frequently in the data; it links the data together; and it explains much of the variation in the data. Basic Social Psychological Processes (BSPs) are a type of core variable that illustrate social processes as they are repeated over time and their detection and explication is an ultimate goal in the writing of grounded theory.

The interview transcripts were analysed by the 'open coding' procedure from grounded theory. Open coding is achieved by what is known as 'the constant comparative method'. This involves a line by line, or even word by word, analysis of the data during which the researcher gives each discrete incident, idea or event a name or code, aiming for the code to be at a higher conceptual level than the text. Proceeding through the text, the researcher generates new codes and finds other examples of already existing codes. Strauss (1987) has detailed the methods whereby codes can be developed in terms of their properties and dimensions by asking questions about their frequency, extent, intensity and duration.

This open coding procedure and the constant comparative method have been described by Glaser and Strauss (1967) as the *sine qua non* of grounded theory methodology. They may thus be contrasted with other qualitative methods within which the coding procedure is claimed to be more predetermined, or at least seen as a 'grid' constructed partly through interaction with the data but also partly from the researcher's original 'set of ideas, prejudices, and mini-theories' (Fleet and Cambourne, 1989).

Level II codes, also known as categories, are derived from condensing level I codes – the open codes. Decisions about categories are made by asking certain questions of the data and then comparing the incident with all others in the field notes or transcripts. The researcher asks what categories other similar incidents would fall into and compares each emerging category with all others to ensure that they are mutually exclusive and cover all the variations. Academic and professional knowledge then supplies theoretical constructs, which may or may not be BSP, to form level III codes, so that they give meaning to the relationship between themselves and the level I and II codes, 'weaving the fractured data back together again' (Glaser, 1978). The comprehensive pattern between these codes is the substantive grounded theory, the theoretical constructs having been grounded in categorical codes rather than being the product of abstract theorizing.

Other sources (Miller, 1994a, 1995a) give a detailed description of the way in which the analysis of these particular transcripts was developed, and a clear account of grounded theory studies in educational settings in general is provided by Hutchinson (1988). The area of investigation – successful interventions with difficult pupil behaviour – is one which, if the study yields positive findings, should have a strong appeal to practitioners working in the field. However, the main purpose of *grounded theory research* is to write new, local theory and this is also presented, as a separate contribution, in Chapter 12.

THE IMPACT OF INTERVENTIONS ON OTHER STAFF

Within grounded theory methodology, the researcher looks in the transcripts for relevant data to fill the emerging categories. This is the process of theoretical sampling which should be taking place while coding proceeds. In this particular study, within a number of the interviews, discussions about teacher colleagues seemed to contain paradoxical and contradictory items and strong feelings. As an aid to developing 'theoretical sensitivity' (Glaser and Strauss, 1967) and in order to be aware of prior biases and expectations, the researcher had, before beginning interviewing, listed a number of possible areas that might yield a rich analysis. The area of relations with colleagues had not been among these and thus it came to be seen as a potential category within which the researcher's theorizing could be extended. Consequently, for the transcripts of later

Table 5.1   Total set of open codes relating to other staff

Pupil impinging on other staff
Role of head
Staff agreement with the need for referral
Consultation within school
School policy on managing the day
Other staff's knowledge of pupil
Previous teachers' strategies with pupil
School culture re problem-solving
Support as the opportunity to talk
Teacher alone/not alone with problem
Staff's/head's support strategy
Reluctance/lack of reluctance to seek support
Valuing/not valuing colleagues' expertise
Staff consensus over presenting problems
Other staff's role in strategy
Consistency of strategy across staff
Individual staff's consistency within strategy
Other staff's knowledge of strategy
Staff's general agreement with strategy
Staff's reluctance re time factors
Staff's reluctance re equitability
Staff's original perception of likelihood of progress
Staff's ongoing perception of progress
Staff's enthusiasm for/interest in strategy

interviews, open coding was first carried out only on sections relating to teacher colleagues.

Also within grounded theory methodology, the analysis of data feeds back into the research design itself, Hammersley and Atkinson (1983) see this as 'the core idea of grounded theorizing ... theory building and data collection are dialectically linked'. As the analysis came to reveal the centrality in the study of issues surrounding colleagues, a new supplementary section was added to the end of the original set of questions, whereby a résumé of the emerging theory was presented to the teachers in the later interviews and their thoughts and comments invited and recorded.

In total, 24 open codes relating to other staff were found to occur and recur within the transcripts and these are listed in Table 5.1. This set of open codes is returned to again for further analysis in Chapter 6, but for the remainder of this chapter a number of common and striking themes which emerged early from the interviews will be presented.

Despite very positive outcomes, many of the teachers were very reluctant to tell their colleagues about the details of the EP's suggestions:

> I was a little unsure and I didn't want to say anything – stick my neck out if you like and say 'Look we're doing this and it could prove wonderful'. I wanted to go very tentatively and then when I could see some sort of hope I turned to the staff and said 'This is what we're doing, will you please bear this in mind.' (Interview 18)

This reticence is being expressed in a school where the general atmosphere is perceived by the teacher as positive – 'a very happy school [where the] staff are very nice and ... all quite happy to help'. The tension between her optimism ('it could prove wonderful') and caution ('I didn't want to say anything – stick my neck out'), a tension present in a dramatic form in many of the interviews, is partly explained by her subsequent comments which reveal something of the texture of staffroom culture:

> I didn't want to offend Margaret [pupil's previous teacher] in any way by saying 'I shall keep him in the class no matter what'. So it was only very gradually that I explained to her what was happening – that's the deputy head ... it's very, very delicate.

Whereas it may be relatively easy to understand this restraint, it is harder to believe that a school staff could perceive positive changes in a pupil with a previously notorious school-wide reputation, be aware that some form of intervention had taken place and yet express little interest in the nature of this intervention. And yet this phenomenon occurs clearly in more than a third of the 24 interviews. The point is perhaps best illustrated by considering sets of three quotes from a number of interviewees, the first in each set being about the previous reputation of the pupil, the second the class teacher's and the other staff's perceptions of change, and the third the staff's curiosity concerning the nature of the intervention responsible for this change.

Interview 13
The other staff were very aware of Brian ... they'd all met him in the playground and in the dining hall.... He would get into trouble with all the other teachers on playground duty and the dinner ladies as well.... He would get very cross and throw himself on the floor and bang his fists on the ground and scream his head off, and he actually did that to the head once, which amazed me. You don't very often do that to the headmaster.

Brian is a changed character. I think everybody's noticed.... I'm absolutely astounded in the change in Brian.

No one's really questioned it as such. They obviously think it's just happened. You tend to take things for granted I suppose if you're not directly involved. No one's actually said to me 'How did you do it?' or whatever.

Interview 20
The parents have had meetings with class teachers, special needs teachers ... throughout the child's stay in school.... She was infamous throughout the school for the things she did.... She had chopped up the duvet cover and the curtains [at home].... We had the Bishop in ... and she went up to his table and sort of 'Oh my name's Chloe!' Most of the other children were quite deferential.

Her behaviour showed, over the last six weeks roughly, a dramatic improvement. Her standard of work did as well and her reading came on in leaps and bounds.... [Staff] who knew I was doing it they'd say 'Ooh she's behaving herself, I didn't have to tell her off in the yard.'

One or two of them did ask me what recommendations she had made, one infant teacher who had her before especially. I didn't make a big issue of it.... If anybody asked I did, but quite honestly at the end of the term it was quite chaotic.

Interview 15
Oh, he had a tremendous reputation, yes ... the chief education officer was at school that day and he cried ... screamed all day ... he was really quite a handful.

He was the topic of conversation in the staffroom but now he's rarely mentioned.... They've remarked how different he's got.

Did they ask what you'd been doing with the ed psych?
No.
Did you tell them?
No, I didn't.

In fact, amongst other staff, some or all were aware of definite improvements in 17 cases, only 1 teacher felt that others were unaware of changes, and 6 did not comment on this aspect.

Although this pattern of a high-profile pupil, a recognition of considerable improvements and a lack of interest in the possible reasons for this is explicit in 9 of the 24 interviews, in many of the remaining cases there is still a clear schism between the teacher's enthusiasm and achievements and the general staff culture. Although the staff are more aware of the nature of the recommended interventions, this does not mean that they are encouraging or positive in their attitude towards them:

Generally the feeling was, why should this child have this sort of treatment ... why should he be seen to be getting special treatment just because he's naughty ...? I think it went against the grain as teachers. (Interview 1)

A lot of people felt that you've got to treat everybody the same.... We had quite a few discussions.... Basically it was 'Well that's all right but are these things fair on the other children?' (Interview 17)

I think we all felt the same. We all felt that maybe ed psychs should come in here and have the class on their own. (Interview 21)

In *only 3 of the 24 interviews* did the teachers feel that the suggested intervention received a positive and encouraging response from their colleagues and then one of these was hedged with a fairly high degree of reservation:

My colleagues were saying 'Yes it probably will work for a few weeks at least.' I think mostly we were reasonably positive that it might hopefully – yes, it would make a difference, but 'what are we going to do after and what's going to happen when it stops working?' (Interview 22)

The combination of having difficulty managing a pupil and

having colleagues who, although supportive in a general sense, were not positive about particular strategies, led to a number of emotional reactions on the part of the teachers interviewed. For some, such as the deputy head from Interview 3, quoted above, the stresses before the EP's intervention were *transferring to their own home lives*. Another said:

> Quite honestly, never having met a child like this in twelve years of teaching, I would go home some days and say 'I don't know what to do next'. (Interview 1)

Additionally, these stresses provoked doubt among some of the teachers about their *professional competence* in general:

> I really was upset because I felt that I was failing, and I mean I've taught for a long time and I can honestly say I've never felt like that before. I just felt that I couldn't cope. (Interview 3)

> You sometimes think will they [colleagues] think it's me, that I'm inadequate? (Interview 21)

A third emotional component, experienced by most of the teachers, was a sense of *feeling alone and solely responsible* for the pupil's behaviour, even in schools where colleagues were seen as generally friendly and supportive. This feeling was conveyed strongly in 10 instances and in a more mixed fashion in another 9:

> It's a fairly strong feeling, you know, you keep your problems in your classroom. (Interview 10)

> I don't think anyone else was that interested to be honest ... he's my problem, Lee. And I don't think anyone thought that much about it. (Interview 14)

> There was a lot of feeling from other [staff] that he shouldn't be [in our school].... When he was naughty in assembly I was the one who always had to fetch him out.... I always had to have him. Nobody ever said to me 'Look I'll take him for you while you get on with what you're supposed to be doing'. (Interview 17)

> I was very aware that the rest of the staff ... would blame Darren for anything because they always have done.... I was having a lot – no, a fair amount of opposition from the head ... any kind of misdemeanour on Darren's part was just jumped on ... you can feel quite isolated in a school. (Interview 18)

It is salutary to note that these strong and pervasive emotional reactions were voiced by a group of teachers whose schools, in the main, possessed or were in the process of developing 'behaviour policies'. In the wake of the Elton Report, there was a popular view that the creation of policies would in itself go a considerable way to ameliorating management problems for individual teachers. These results provide unsettling evidence that this may be far from the truth. (The subject of behaviour policies will be returned to in Chapter 6.)

In summary, then, in only 2 of the 24 cases did the teachers not feel that their colleagues were either uninterested in their actions, negative about the EP's recommendations or doubtful about the likelihood of their success.

However, in working with the EP a totally contrasting sense of supportive attention is relayed in many of the interviews:

> I think he was seeing it as I was. I think he was seeing that I just couldn't take any more.... I suppose he had the authority to make suggestions and he also in a way was taking some of the responsibility I suppose and it was nothing to do with the rest of the staff really. They just breathed a sigh of relief that it wasn't their problem. (Interview 3)

> She didn't quiz me. She was lovely, she would just sit there and I could ask her questions, like 'I am trying this particular thing, is that all right?'.... She would sort of say 'You're doing well, yes you are doing the right thing'. So yes, I appreciated that part of her ... as the professional.... [The other teachers] would have said.... 'Oh go on, he'll be all right' ... but it meant more coming from her.... She was trying hard to get Brian out of this negative situation. (Interview 15)

Within the 24 interventions investigated, 18 resulted in teachers and parents working in some form of partnership. In many of these the EP's contribution to the formation and/or direction of this working relationship is readily apparent. In some, the EP's effect, in terms of teachers feeling legitimized to operate in a different way, is very much present even when the EP himself or herself is not actually physically present, as the following excerpt illustrates:

> Theresa (EP) also suggested talking to the parents as well.
>
> *Had you not done that before?*
>
> Yes, I'd spoken to them in an informal way but not actually had them in and talked to them formally. She recommends that a lot.
>
> *Did she suggest any particular things to say to Gary's parents?*
>
> Yes, to try to stress the positive side of Gary, and the head and I had a very interesting chat....
>
> (Later)
>
> *Do you think you would have got to know the parents anyway like that or do you think it was because Theresa suggested these things*

that it helped you to get to know the parents better?

I think maybe it was a little bit of both. We see the parents at the beginning of the day for five minutes, five minutes at the end, but when we had that formal interview with the head, myself and the parents, I think we got a lot more into the background, that maybe she wouldn't have said as much – they wouldn't have said as much just picking the child up. So we got to know a little bit more of what it was like at home and that was one of Theresa's suggestions. (Interview 7)

In the usual sense of the word, procedures that are *formal* could be invoked by a school if, for example, suspension of a pupil was being considered or an assessment made of special educational needs within the Code of Practice. However, there is no reference in the interview to any procedures of this nature. Instead, the term is used here as a frequent reminder that the head and the teacher are behaving untypically, 'delving into home backgrounds', and that this has apparently been recommended by the EP. Presumably they are quite capable of asking such questions of their own volition and of giving advice concerning praise and encouragement. There is nothing particularly 'expert' about either. Similarly, if the parents were to take great exception to this, it seems highly unlikely that justifying themselves by saying they were acting on the EP's suggestions would save them from the immediacy of the parents' anger.

The EP's influence appears to remain in an almost reified form to govern the interactions taking place, which are clearly perceived as a departure from the normal form of interaction that takes place between parents and teachers when there is a difficulty associated with a pupil's behaviour. Just as some of the teachers experienced a sense of supportive attention from their EP that contrasted so sharply with their colleagues' response to the negotiated strategy, so too they were aware of construing some parents anew in a way that departed from normal school procedures:

Mrs Roberts [mother] had caused so many problems here. She's a very bristly lady, very much on the ball, but in her own way she really did care for Barry. Maybe not the way that you and I would care for our children but she did ... she really was a caring mum. (Interview 15)

The involvement of the EP in some way allows the generally accepted view amongst the staff, that Mrs Roberts is very 'bristly' and causes 'so many problems', to be departed from but continue to coexist with a more positive, if perhaps patronizing, view of her as a 'caring mum'. This temporary escape from the dominant view is also sometimes expressed in terms of privacy and ownership:

> I think a lot of the time when teachers are working with a psychologist they keep it very much to – it's their property almost. It's strange ... teachers are very possessive of the children in their class and they don't want to share things. (Interview 24)

This phenomenological experience of 'possessiveness' and secrecy, of not 'sticking one's neck out', may be understandable in the example from Interview 18 in which the teacher initially found the prospect of success after the relative 'failure' of the deputy head in the previous year 'very, very delicate'. The likelihood of major changes in a certain pupil's behaviour is not a feature within the discourse of the majority (or any) of the other staff. Even after successful completion, when the results are visible to the others in the school, the notions of teacher-effected change with difficult pupils will not fit easily into the staff culture:

> I mean I've come back to teaching after 15 years' break and they've been super, they've been really helpful.... I can't come in [to the staffroom] and say 'Aren't I good?'... It's very big-headed isn't it? (Interview 15)

> We're a very close school ... we do talk in the staffroom and say, you know, 'What do you think? How can you help?' ... [when] I found that it was working then I thought that as I felt so good about it everybody had to know.... I think they all got fed up of me keep saying 'Richard, Richard, Richard!' (Interview 21)

The analysis so far has identified and explored to some extent the discouraging reactions of colleagues to a teacher's successful interventions. It has contrasted this with very different working relationships with EPs and identified a changed style of interacting with parents.

In order to pursue the analysis of these phenomena at a more detailed theoretical level, it is necessary in the next chapter to return to the literature, to engage in a greater level of theoretical sensitivity in the area of relationships with colleagues and organizational dynamics in general. From this position the present level I data on colleagues, displayed in Table 5.1, can be coded at levels II and III and the data then questioned further in order to discover the relationship between these and other significant emerging categories.

CHAPTER 6

Teachers as colleagues: the paradox of sympathetic support

The preliminary analysis of the interview transcripts reported in Chapter 5 identified two major strands for further investigation: firstly, the apparent paradox of teacher colleagues who are experienced as generally supportive but also display a seemingly determined lack of interest in the nature of successful teacher strategies; and secondly, the processes whereby EPs bring teachers and parents into a working relationship that proves far more productive than previous attempts not involving a consultant. Whilst further coding of transcripts and more probing questioning took place in later interviews, additional theoretical sensitivity was pursued by means of a literature search that concentrated upon deepening the researcher's appreciation of probable related topics.

In particular, these consisted of

- organizations and cultures;
- individual teachers and schools as organizations and cultures;
- systems and their boundaries.

This chapter consists of brief reviews of these areas in preparation for a more detailed and more theoretically sensitive analysis of the transcripts.

ORGANIZATIONS AND CULTURES

Henning-Stout and Conoley (1988) have argued that the success of a consultant working with a school depends equally upon the characteristics of the consultant and those of the organization. They identified three aspects of an organization that are implicated in the outcomes of consultative practice: the organization's history with previous consultants, organizational stresses, and the prevailing ideology of the organization. These are factors usually found in discussions about the properties of systems and the interactions across their boundaries (e.g. Glatter, 1989), with the literature on organizational cultures (Morgan, 1986) and with teacher cultures specifically (Woods, 1984; Hammersley, 1984).

The culture of a school has been described by Dalin (1993) as 'what we experience as the "way things are" in an organisation, the written and unwritten rules that regulate behaviour, the stories and the "myths" of what an organisation has achieved, the standards and the values set for its members'. Deal and Kennedy (1982) have put it more simply as the 'system of informal rules that spells out how people are to behave most of the time'. This may obviously be compared and possibly contrasted with the various public pronouncements or policies that purport to describe how an organization is structured and functions. Argyris and Schon (1978) have referred to these two phenomena as 'theory in use' and 'espoused theory' respectively, and have claimed that one of the most important steps in understanding an organization is the detection of the possible gaps between its espoused theory and its theory-in-use. Argyris and Schon point out that organizations are extremely well practised and effective in 'defensive routines' when there is any possibility of a gap between their espoused theory and their theory-in-use being revealed.

Although ethnographic research in schools has mainly been concerned with classroom practice and therefore focused on observation and interview methods, a few researchers have looked particularly at staffrooms. Woods (1984) examined the nature and function of staffroom humour and Hammersley (1984) looked at the subject of staffroom 'news'.

In the latter study, Hammersley found that staffroom news

served both a referential and a rhetorical function. Because this work was carried out in a secondary school, in which pupils move from teacher to teacher, staffroom conversations gave teachers the opportunity to know what to expect from particular pupils. Hammersley found that the conversation focused predominantly on the difficult behaviour of pupils and consisted of the trading of summary typifications. Because teachers employ typifications of pupils to guide their actions in the immediacy of the classrooms, Hammersley argued that through the exchange of classroom news teachers supplement their own information with that of colleagues in the construction of these typifications.

However, Hammersley also detected aspects of teacher conversations that served a dismissive rather than a descriptive function. In this rhetorical form, conversations were concerned with hypothesized characteristics of particular pupils rather than detailed descriptions of their behaviour. Hammersley found that in all the examples of conversation he collected, the context of any pupil behaviour – that is, the setting, the teacher's expectations and actions, etc. – was taken for granted and did not need explanation or discussion in terms of its possible contribution to pupil behaviour. The recurrent topic for comment and discussion in the staffroom was the 'failure' of pupils in various contexts, a failure seen as due to the typifications given to pupils by the teachers. These typifications, consisting of psychological characteristics, were such that they could be seen to produce typical behaviour in diverse contexts, irrespective of the contexts themselves.

INDIVIDUAL TEACHERS AND SCHOOLS AS ORGANIZATIONS AND CULTURES

A number of commentators have drawn attention to the sense of isolation that characterizes the professional role of the teacher. For example, Lieberman and Miller (1990), writing about the American scene, have stated that

> loneliness and isolation are high prices to pay but teachers willingly pay them when the alternatives are seen as exposure and censure.... By following the privacy rule teachers forfeit the oppor-

tunity to display their successes; but they also gain. They gain the security of not having to face their failures publicly and losing face.

Similarly, Little (1990), reviewing studies of teachers working in a 'collegial' manner, also sees 'a devastating picture of professional isolation among experienced teachers and trial and error survival of beginning teachers'. She does find examples of genuine peer support and joint effort but concludes that it is 'a remarkable accomplishment: not the rule, but the rare, often fragile exception'.

It is not that teachers do not necessarily enjoy the company of their colleagues but rather that colleagues do not serve the function of being stimuli and agents for one another's professional development. 'Many teachers are satisfied with their peer relationships, but few claim that those relationships make their way into the classroom. Many schools offer congenial work environments, but few offer a professional environment that makes schools as educative for teachers as for students' (Little, 1990).

This point was dealt with at greater length by Lortie (1975) in his sociological study of teaching. He referred to the ambivalence for the teacher, in respect of colleagues, between what he called 'the wish for boundedness and the search for assistance'. Lortie discovered in his study that the major reward for teachers was in the form of interactions with *their* pupils and satisfaction with their learning and development. Although various administrative duties – lunchtime supervision, etc. – were seen as requiring collaborative efforts between teachers from the point of view of equitability, these 'costs' were balanced by the 'profits of psychic benefits' from working alone with pupils. Lortie describes teachers as 'entrepreneurs of psychic profit' working to maximize positive interactions and feedback from their pupils, whilst attempting to reduce the organization's influence on them and ensure that they have no more bosses than already exist.

However, these teachers also reported that they saw their colleagues as a powerful source of ideas and, sometimes, as mirrors in which to assess their own performance. Lortie's analysis, much more than the previous two papers, sees teachers as more positively involved in maintaining the boundedness of some important arenas of their work despite the cost of professional isolation.

These three papers identify a number of factors that contribute to this phenomenon:

- the ecology of most schools, with their separated class-rooms;
- the major reward for teachers, the development and responses of pupils, being something most easily earned away from colleagues;
- the lack of a technical language with which teachers can discuss their work with each other;
- the lack of commonly agreed standards by which teachers can measure their competence, leading to a lack of confidence through an inability to judge their own worth;
- the high value placed upon being able to keep a class under control, leading both to a wariness of being observed and a desire to keep a class within a more bounded space where it can be more easily managed.

Sharp and Green (1975), in their ethnographic study of a 'progressive' primary school, argued that teachers utilized a 'child-centred vocabulary' to account for their classroom actions to significant others but that these actions were themselves guided far more by the principle of 'ad-hocing' and following tried and tested routines to cope with the immediacy, frequency and changing nature of classroom demands. In such circumstances, even if teachers possessed a shared technical language in the form of the child-centred vocabulary, the fact that it did not link to their actions can clearly cause a situation in which conversations with colleagues about purposes and methods grounded in practice could become extremely difficult.

Despite these barriers to a shared professional culture, teachers need reference groups from which to derive norms and values for their practice. Nias (1985) examined the function of reference groups by interviewing 99 teachers from various parts of England who had been teaching for between 2 and 9 years. In particular she was concerned with the role of reference groups in the defence of the self, both through a normative function in which individuals identify a group against whose norms and values they wish to evaluate themselves, and through a perceptual function whereby the group's norms are used as anchoring points in structuring the perceptual field. 'Thus once one has internalised the particular outlook of a reference group, it becomes a "frame of reference" which is brought to bear on all new situations' (p. 107).

Many of the teachers appeared to need the referential support from only one other, either a colleague, headteacher or a visiting professional. Nias comments that the amount of support provided by such a group was out of all proportion to either the size of the group or the time spent in communication. Also, the majority of teachers interviewed found themselves at some stage working in schools where they had no adult reference group and then they often sought it in outside courses or from 'like-minded' friends. Interestingly, especially in respect of Lortie's findings concerning the primary rewards for teachers, the most frequently invoked reference group in Nias's study was pupils. In other words, they were the group whose positive reactions the teachers claimed to be most concerned to meet. 'As long as classroom processes remain largely hidden from all other participants, pupils may be invoked as a reference group to justify many different decisions and types of behaviour' (p. 109).

Nias extends Lortie's argument concerning the lack of a common technical culture and language among teachers. She considers that teachers construct their views of themselves and of reality within schools via conversations with their own reference groups. Outside these groups they do not share a language with which to attach meanings to their common experience. Attempting to create such a language with others outside the reference group would actually be destructive of the processes which create and sustain their substantial selves. Hence, teachers actively do not enter into conversation about fundamental aspects of their work with many of their colleagues.

However, it is recognized that teachers also have certain affiliative and affective needs in respect of their colleagues 'especially in circumstances where they feel themselves to be under threat from pupils'. Consequently, open conflict is often avoided by arriving at a 'false consensus' in the staffroom while the teacher continues to follow a course of action in the classroom more consistent with the norms of a reference group.

Drawing together a range of perspectives, including rational–emotive therapy and cognitive behaviour therapy, Wagner (1987) has developed the model of the 'knot' in teacher thinking. This is the situation when the dominance of 'self-imperated cognitions' – beliefs and messages to oneself couched in the form of 'shoulds, musts and oughts' – prevents a form of thinking that leads to problem-solving. As part of a six-year study in Germany, Wagner showed how teachers' thinking was often characterized by going 'round in circles, posing questions without resolving them, jumping from one issue to another and considering goals and strategies without ever putting them into practice'. Most importantly, and this was found to be a dominant feature of knots, there appeared to be no recognition of the many contradictions contained in these modes of thought. The other consequence was a strong emotional component, often involving anger, anxiety or attachment, and seen as the result of vain attempts to resolve these dilemmas or knots.

One section of the study most pertinent to this discussion concerned the in-depth analysis, using an original methodology, of the knots occurring in the transcripts from interviews with 7 teachers about their school life. There were 62 issues that teachers talked about at least 12 times or more and 4 that contained significantly more knots than the others. Surprisingly, these were 'fellow teachers' (83 per cent), the principal (81 per cent), giving permission as opposed to forbidding students to do certain things (70 per cent), students paying attention rather than being absent-minded or distracted (65 per cent). The issue that produced the fewest knots was the actual content or subject matter of the teaching.

In other words, issues relating to immediate teacher colleagues produced more inconsequential and contradictory thinking, with high levels of emotional components, than did either the curriculum or even pupil management aspects of work.

SYSTEMS AND THEIR BOUNDARIES

There has been considerable interest in systems theory approaches amongst those who have studied schools as organizations. Hoy and Miskel (1989), for example, described schools as open systems interacting with their environments, and discussed the ways in which uncertainty in the environment affects the internal structures and processes of organizations. Similarly, Rice (1976), discussing open or 'socio-technical' systems, described how systems seek to define, or validate, and then maintain a definition of their boundary during transactions across it with the environment.

The purpose of the boundary is to distinguish those tasks and responsibilities belonging to the system from those that do not. Within a system's boundary, norms and procedures are then arrived at to guide such activities as interacting with others inside the system, dealing with internally disruptive events, carrying out joint tasks, presenting the system's stated aims and objectives to the environment, and communicating across the boundary.

In addition to boundary validation and maintenance, another important aspect of systems is their orientation towards homeostasis, a tendency to maintain internal stability. Systemic family therapy (Palazzoli *et al.*, 1978) has drawn upon similar theoretical roots, with the nature of the boundary, its maintenance and the interactions that take place across it, again yielding important conceptual tools to inform the practice of therapists. A particularly significant notion deriving from systemic family therapy is that of 'the rules about the rules' – the principles, often informally defined and communicated, concerning who is permitted, and by what means, to generate, challenge, change and make exceptions to the norms and procedures of the system.

In the context of family therapy, De Shazer (1982) has argued that 'when the system under consideration is defined as the open system of the therapy situation, then the boundary is drawn around the therapist and the family subsystems of the therapeutic suprasystems'. This new system then develops its own norms and values but is temporary in the sense that its existence depends on the continuance of the therapist's involvement.

Quicke (1982) was critical of early systems approaches within the profession of educational psychology, despite welcoming them as an alternative to what he saw as the limited nature of the professional casework that preceded them. He challenges Burden's early systems work for paying scant attention to the 'hidden curriculum' of schools and the procedures whereby cultural norms are established, preferring to concentrate instead on formal and explicitly stated structures. Ball (1987) has also criticized systems approaches and accused their adherents of bypassing and obscuring the realities of organizational life in schools in favour of 'the abstract tidiness of conceptual debate'. Instead, he advocated that schools as organizations would be better understood through the study of 'the micro-politics of school life'.

Frederickson (1990) has helped clarify this discussion by pointing to the confusingly broad range of professional practice that has often been uncritically included under the rubric of 'systems approaches'. Particularly helpful here is her distinction between systems theories which derive by analogy from a biological perspective, such as those employed in systemic family therapy and the socio-technical approach, and those having their origins in a technological perspective, for example, soft systems and hard systems methodology.

Hard systems methodology is the area concerned with work addressing the formal structure of organizations, as developed within professional educational psychology by Burden (see Chapter 7). It is the biological tradition which gives rise to concepts such as boundary maintenance and homeostasis, concepts which, as Frederickson points out, can elucidate processes within organizations by analogy but which should not be developed too literally.

So far, this chapter has identified a number of processes relating to schools as organizations and cultures which may be implicated in ambiguous and problematic relationships between teacher colleagues in the context of difficult pupil behaviour. Similarly, systems theory derived from a biological perspective may also offer conceptual tools with which to elucidate those factors influencing the interactions that take place between teachers and parents in such circumstances. With this theoretical sensitivity, the transcripts were further examined to allow categorization and theory building to proceed.

A further analysis of the level I codes relating to 'other staff' (see Table 5.1) enabled two major categories to be derived at a relatively early stage. These could be identified as the espoused theory and the theory-in-use as far as the responses of these schools to difficult pupil behaviour were concerned. The former was often manifested in the form of a written policy document, whereas the latter was often referred to much in the manner of

Deal and Kennedy's (1982) definition of staff culture, 'the system of informal rules that spells out how people are to behave most of the time'. The derivation of these categories, by a process of level II and III coding and sorting, is shown in diagrammatic form in Figure 6.2, later in this chapter.

Developing further the partial sense of isolation from colleagues experienced by the teachers in this study and described in Chapter 5, it is possible to detect in almost all the transcripts a conflict within the relationship between espoused theory (policy), theory-in-use (culture) and the teacher's preferred method of handling the pupil.

POLICY–CULTURE CONFLICT

For the schools in this study, 14 were said to have a written policy concerning behaviour, 6 were in the process of developing one, and 4 were without such plans as far as the interviewee was aware. In this study, the term 'policy' is taken to include both written statements accessible to the staff and less clearly articulated procedures that are generally recognized as institutionally approved, usually by originating from the head or other policy-maker.

Even in a number of the schools with explicit policies, teachers were still able to identify prevailing attitudes and assumptions of the staff – the staff culture – as being incompatible with the formally expressed policy. For example, one of the special needs co-ordinators, in a school with a written behaviour policy, said

> we started a system of rewards ... in the school generally, yet, at the same time, I felt guilty that these problems [a particular pupil's difficult behaviour] simply weren't being addressed and that it was down to me in my role and the class teacher. (Interview 5)

A number of interviewees described the procedure whereby teachers with a difficult pupil would consult with either the head or the special needs teacher;

> I think if I had a real problem with a child I would see the head and then she would say 'Well try this ... have you tried that?' Or she would say 'Right, we'll call in the ed psych.' (Interview 9)

> I normally go to Rachel (SEN Co-ordinator) for help and advice on

problems like this one. I spoke to her originally and said 'Look I've got a real problem here and I need some help' and she tried to give me some help. (Interview 13)

However, despite the existence and recognition of such procedures, the staff culture, in these same cases, lies in marked contrast to this problem-solving and advice-giving approach:

I think that sometimes you just get in the staffroom and think, you know, you don't want to talk. I mean really you just want to moan about your children, you don't want anyone to tell you anything because you don't want to listen. You just want to get it out of your system. (Interview 9)

I think a lot of the time when we talk to each other in the staffroom we can be a bit negative, you know, doomy about things. We don't always make each other feel 'Go on, you can do it!' (Interview 13)

In these examples the teachers have a positive attitude towards the formal policy but at the same time experience an unsupportive culture, unsupportive in the sense of not taking a positive approach towards a difficult pupil. In other examples the reverse is the case: the official way of dealing with difficult behaviour is not highly regarded but the informal support received from colleagues is positively experienced.

For example, one teacher describes her opposition to the headteacher's preferred method of dealing with a particular pupil:

I fought very strongly because the head ... just wanted him removed. (Interview 18)

Although the rest of the staff were described as having lost much of their patience with this boy, the culture is nevertheless perceived as positive:

This is a very happy school and the staff are very nice indeed and they were all quite happy to help. (Interview 18)

To summarize this section, for these particular teachers there was seen to be in 8 cases a tension between culture and school policy, whether it was in a written form or not, no tension in 6, and an indeterminate relationship in 10. Any actions on the part of a teacher that were likely to point out this disparity between espoused theory and theory-in-use would be likely to be met by one of the organization's 'well-practiced defensive routines' (Argyris and Schon, 1978).

POLICY–TEACHER CONFLICTS

In other interviews it was possible to detect a strain between the school's formal procedures and the teacher's preferred method, without there necessarily being such a clear or obvious clash between policy and culture. A deputy head who had taught for 25 years described her reaction to the strategy of placing a difficult pupil in her class because of her seniority and experience:

> Well the head – I think she just thought 'Well I know you'll cope' you know. Well I didn't. In fact, I could cope but I just went in saying I'm not prepared to any more ... I really did feel that as long as I coped I could be left to do it ... In fact people used to send him out from things, out of assembly or a story, and back to me. (Interview 3)

Another teacher who did not feel comfortable with the school's procedure for approaching difficult behaviour said:

> Now the head communicates very, very well but she communicates only with the person she needs to communicate with. She doesn't communicate generally in the staffroom if there's a problem with the children and really we don't delve into backgrounds too much. If it's necessary we do.... Maybe my one criticism would be that it [the school] is very, very secretive. (Interview 7)

Whilst this criticism is rather guarded and set within a generally positive approach towards the main policy-maker – the head – other teachers expressed their disagreement in stronger terms:

> The head ... knew the best way to do it and he would have him in his office working at a little table but then all of a sudden he'd have to go to a meeting so he'd have to pile him on to someone else or he'd have the odd private phone call or show someone around the school so Darren was left by himself in the office.... You don't discuss it with the head, he hasn't got a clue.... In our school you don't send them to the head because it just causes more hassle for you. (Interview 16)

In the remaining interviews 6 teachers indicated weak strains in relation to policy (making 9 in total who experienced a negative reaction to the school policy), 8 (one of them a teaching head, and two special needs co-ordinators) described their policy in either a positive or non-judgemental fashion and the remaining 7 made no reference to standard procedures in relation to difficult behaviour.

Thus strains in the relationship between policy and the

teacher may be seen to be a factor in 9 of the 24 cases, and a powerful one in 3 of these.

CULTURE–TEACHER CONFLICTS

The general culture of a school may be positively perceived by a teacher, irrespective of any prevailing views specifically concerning difficult behaviour, and this was the case in 10 interviews. In these positive instances comments were usually very general and to the effect that the school was 'very happy' or 'open' and that staff very 'supportive' or 'sympathetic'.

Negative views of the culture usually existed where the teacher felt that a rejecting or 'doomy' attitude prevailed in relation to difficult pupils (as in Interviews 9 and 13 above). The teachers in the study perceived this as clashing with the positive approach they were trying to adopt with the pupil in question.

However, these attitudes were expressed more intensely in some of the sample:

> [The staff] felt they [difficult children] shouldn't be here if they're going to behave like that ... they should be somewhere else. (Interview 17)

> They thought that he was really a lost cause and they thought he was extremely obnoxious and aggressive and a very naughty boy.... His previous teacher was still smarting quite badly from his behaviour. (Interview 18)

Whereas here the culture is being created and maintained by the staff's verbal reactions, it is possible for it to be communicated in equally powerful but far less tangible ways:

> I've gone in as an acting deputy in lots of different schools ... and [in] several schools I've been in it's 'The children are in your class, your responsibility, you look after them, you deal with them, if there's a problem you handle it.'

> *Who's saying that?*

> Oh no, it's *there* when you walk through the door

> *So nobody's actually saying it?*

> No, it's *there*. (Interview 24)

Even though a negative general culture was only perceived in 6 cases, none the less, a sense of feeling alone with the responsibility for a pupil's difficult behaviour was to be found throughout many of the interviews. It was stated strongly in 10 instances, and in a more mixed fashion in 9. The following examples are all from schools where the general culture is perceived as positive.

> People need to know, really do need to know, that they're not bad teachers. I needed to know that after twelve years I wasn't being gotten the better of by a five-year-old child. (Interview 1)

> You always do as a teacher tend to think it's your fault. (Interview 3)

> They all thought I was fighting a losing battle. (Interview 15)

> You sometimes think 'Will they [colleagues] think it's me, I'm inadequate?' (Interview 21)

In summary, the teacher perceived the *general* school culture to be negative in 6 cases, positive in 10, and a mixture of both in 3. In only 4 cases was no judgement conveyed. However, as far as the culture specifically in regard to difficult pupils is concerned, there was a widespread feeling among the teachers interviewed of being solely responsible for the solution, and sometimes for the causes of a pupil's problem behaviour.

THE CREATION OF A TEMPORARY OVERLAPPING SYSTEM

In total, in only 3 of the 24 cases were there seen to be no initial strains in the relationship between policy, culture and the teacher's view in respect of a particular difficult pupil. It is important to emphasize that this does not mean that the schools were in a perpetual state of disharmony. What it does mean is that when the teachers in this study found themselves with a difficult pupil, then, from their perspective, there was an internal strain within the system. If there was no intervention then homeostasis could be restored either by changes in policy, in culture or in the teacher's attitude towards the pupil in question.

Change in policy requires the time and commitment of a large number of staff and is unlikely to result as a response to a single pupil. Change in culture, by definition, is extremely difficult to arrange even if time and commitment are available. For a particular teacher, holding attitudes or acting contrary to policy and/or culture in the fraught area of extreme pupil behaviour, however, would normally lead inevitably to increasing alienation. Yet this does not occur in these interviews. So what processes are at work encouraging positive outcomes for the teacher and child whilst at the same time avoiding an increase in internal strains?

The interviews reveal a frequent teacher perception of a temporary and overlapping system deriving from the involvement of the EP. This system always includes the teacher, pupil, EP and mother and often also contains other family members and staff, particularly dinner supervisors and non-teaching assistants. It takes the form of the 'therapeutic suprasystem' described by De Shazer (1982) in the context of family therapy, in which the boundary is drawn around both the family and the therapist to create a new system. This new system develops its own norms and values but is temporary in the sense that its existence depends on the continuance of the therapist's involvement.

In these interviews, the new system is seen as temporary (see Figure 6.1); it originates with the 'formal' involvement of the EP and it ceases with the ending of this involvement. Whilst the system is in place it allows the teachers to step outside the values and norms of behaviour imposed through membership of the school system. Looking again at two of the quotes used in chapter 5, it is possible to illustrate some aspects of this new boundary, perceived by the teachers as a seemingly paradoxical combination of the fragile and intangible with the authoritative and reassuring.

> I think he [EP] was seeing it as I was. I think he was seeing that I just couldn't take any more.... I suppose he had the authority to make suggestions and he also in a way was taking some of the responsibility I suppose and it was nothing to do with the rest of the staff really. They just breathed a sigh of relief that it wasn't their problem. (Interview 3)

> She didn't quiz me. She was lovely, she would just sit there and I could ask her questions, like 'I am trying this particular thing, is that all right?'... She would sort of say 'You're doing well, yes you are doing the right thing.' So yes, I appreciated that part of her ... as the professional.... [The other teachers] would have said ... 'Oh go on, he'll be all right' ... but it meant more coming from her.... She was trying hard to get Brian out of this negative situation. (Interview 15)

'She didn't quiz me ... she was lovely' is language more appropriate to a reference group (Nias, 1985), and many of these

Figure 6.1   The location and nature of the temporary overlapping boundary. (a) The child as a member of the family and school systems; (b) the introduction of the temporary overlapping system.

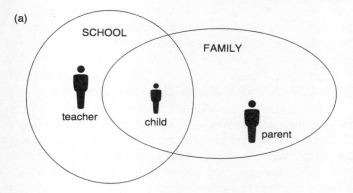

(a)

Each boundary includes the norms and rules for:

• interacting with individuals within the system
• dealing with internally disruptive events
• carrying out joint tasks
• presenting a 'common front'
• communicating across the boundary

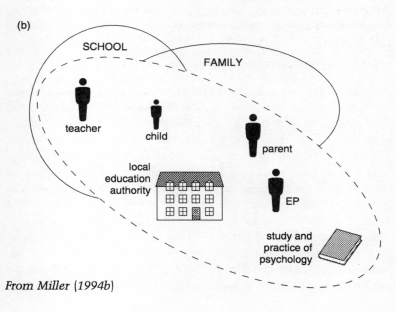

(b)

From Miller (1994b)

teachers' accounts of working with the EP are couched in similar terms. Within this new system, the norms and support of a reference group allow the teachers to construe pupils and parents differently, to escape from the typifications identified by Hammersley (1984) in which difficult behaviour was seen only in terms of fixed personality characteristics.

SYSTEMS BOUNDARY MAINTENANCE

The new temporary boundary achieves two functions. Firstly, it defines a new system within which norms and expectations more typical of a reference group can be encouraged. Usually this new system includes at least the teacher, the mother and the EP. In a minority of cases the system comprises only the teacher and the EP but the same degree of intersubjectivity can still be detected in these accounts. As a result of these new norms it becomes possible to reconstrue children and parents. In discussing family therapy procedures, Dallos (1991) comments that

> a dialectical approach ... emphasises repeatedly that action and construing are inextricably connected.... Change involves a shift at both levels – action and construing ... we need to be wary when there is only evidence of movement in one area and not the other. It is easy enough to talk about things in a different way and to act in a different way, at least for a while. However, in order for change to be sustained, shifts in both areas are necessary. (p. 142)

Not only, then, does the new system create a partnership which will implement a joint strategy, it also creates a level of personal relationship within which it is possible for members to reconstrue each other, thus adding to the strategy itself in the manner Dallos sees as essential for sustained change within a system.

However, the temporary boundary also serves a function in respect of one of the major systems, the school. Normally, transgression of the rules and norms of the major system would lead to an increased internal strain – a decrease in homeostasis – within that system. But the new procedures are seen to exist only for the life of the temporary system. When it is removed, when the mechanism that brought it into being, the 'official' involvement of the EP, ceases to operate, the major boundary of the school system with its norms and procedures can be seen to have been preserved intact. Even when not physically present, the EP was still seen as responsible for the temporarily new way of responding to pupils and parents.

The school system will preserve its set of norms concerning the extent of tolerable difficult behaviour and the procedures for relating with parents in circumstances where it seems as though dialogue has broken down. Although the experiences of the teachers in this study will have demonstrated that their own actions, aided and mediated by an outside consultant, can have a very positive effect even in extreme circumstances, the need to protect both policy and culture remains. As these reflect the boundary of a system's responsibilities in uncertain relations with its environment (Rice, 1976), they serve to increase internal collegiate support in times of professional threat. The nature of future threats is unpredictable; therefore it is unlikely that the experience of one particular case will lead to the teacher involved making great efforts to disrupt the system's homeostasis by pushing for new school procedures, permanently altering the location of the boundary because of one particular event.

Consequently, the lack of interest on the part of the rest of the staff may not originate solely from them. For the teacher in question to bring into the staffroom accounts of teacher-initiated change would threaten the organization's homeostasis, hence the teachers in this study would be as likely to 'talk down' their achievements in order to preserve affiliative links with colleagues as the rest of the staff would be diffident in enquiring about them. The teacher also avoids being on the receiving end of the organization's 'defensive routines' by not highlighting any mismatch between espoused theory and theory-in-use in relation to problem behaviour. The intervention can be accommodated precisely because it is separated and distinct from the activities of the major system. The school has maintained its boundary, changes in policy, culture or practice have not been required, nor have possible inconsistencies between them been illuminated.

Figure 6.2 shows the higher level coding and categorization of the level I codes relating to 'other staff'. Developed in interaction with the theoretical literature, this process of categorization and sorting leads to the emergence of 'boundary maintenance' as a

Figure 6.2 The relationship between levels I, II and III codes relating to 'other staff'

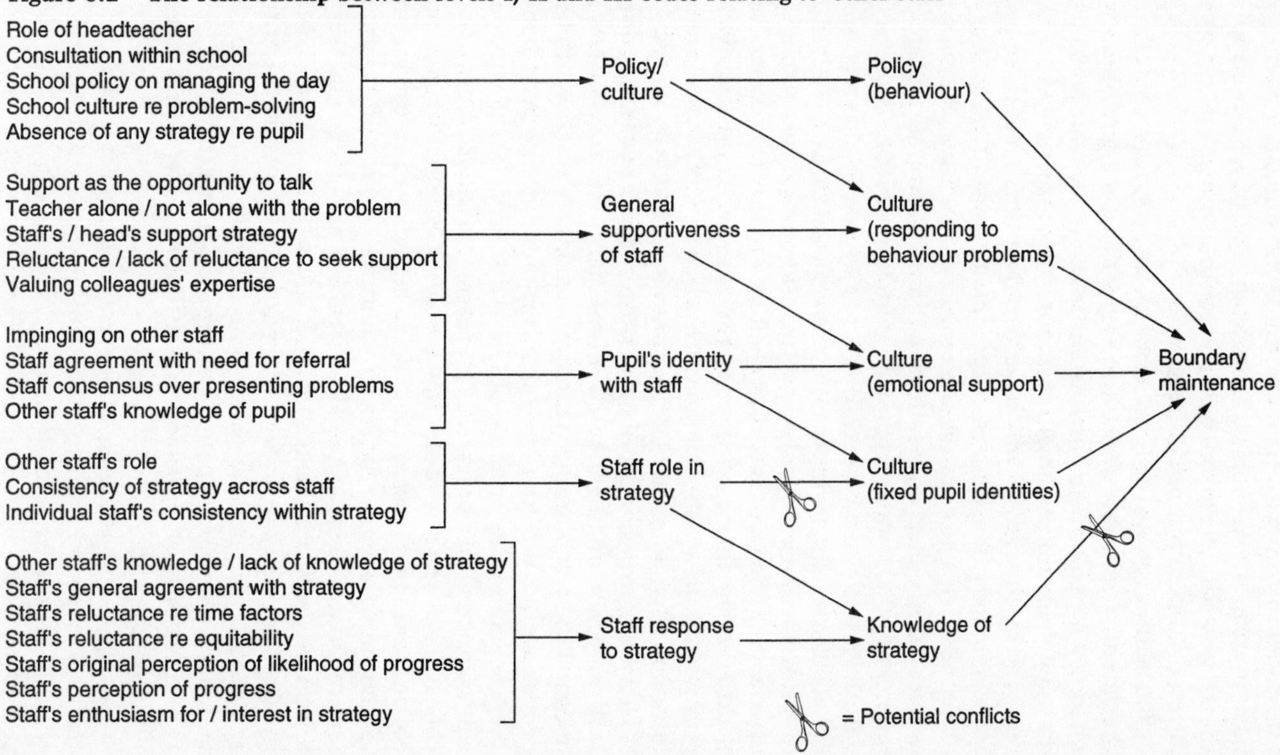

Role of headteacher
Consultation within school
School policy on managing the day
School culture re problem-solving
Absence of any strategy re pupil

→ Policy/culture → Policy (behaviour) → Boundary maintenance

Support as the opportunity to talk
Teacher alone / not alone with the problem
Staff's / head's support strategy
Reluctance / lack of reluctance to seek support
Valuing colleagues' expertise

→ General supportiveness of staff → Culture (responding to behaviour problems)

Impinging on other staff
Staff agreement with need for referral
Staff consensus over presenting problems
Other staff's knowledge of pupil

→ Pupil's identity with staff → Culture (emotional support)

Other staff's role
Consistency of strategy across staff
Individual staff's consistency within strategy

→ Staff role in strategy → Culture (fixed pupil identities)

Other staff's knowledge / lack of knowledge of strategy
Staff's general agreement with strategy
Staff's reluctance re time factors
Staff's reluctance re equitability
Staff's original perception of likelihood of progress
Staff's perception of progress
Staff's enthusiasm for / interest in strategy

→ Staff response to strategy → Knowledge of strategy

✂ = Potential conflicts

core variable or, in Glaser's (1978) terminology, a Basic Social Psychological Process. This core variable appears to satisfy Glaser's three criteria of recurring frequently in the data (that is, the data concerning 'other staff' rather than the full transcripts), linking the data together, and explaining much of the variation within the data. Figure 6.2 also illustrates that there are two areas that are likely to threaten the relationship between these codes, and hence the 'boundary maintenance' variable itself: too great a role for other staff in the strategy, which would disrupt the process of shared typifications of deviant pupils; and too much knowledge of the strategy and its effectiveness on the part of other staff, which could lead to a tension with the culture and policy in relation to managing difficult behaviour.

The literature reviewed in Chapter 4 of this study has revealed quite clearly that many teachers have displayed considerable reservations about behavioural approaches, both originally in the early 1970s and more recently, and in both Britain and the United States. If the analysis so far in terms of organizational dynamics has offered an explanation for this slow take-up despite numerous successful case examples, then the remainder of this study could be profitably turned towards a more detailed examination of the factors that encouraged and then sustained the participation of the teachers in this particular study.

CHAPTER 7

Defining the successful consultation

A useful starting point in the attempt to understand those instances of successful collaborative work between teachers and EPs is the topic area of 'consultation'. This chapter will consider consultative practice, especially in relation to pupil behaviour, and attempt to link together professional developments, other empirical research and the data gathered in the present study.

MODELS OF CONSULTATION

A number of writers have offered definitions of the term 'consultation'. Conoley and Conoley (1990) describe it as a problem-solving relationship between professionals from different fields, having aspects in common with psychotherapy and advice-giving. Unlike psychotherapy, however, they argue that consultation only focuses upon work-related problems and avoids 'intrapsychic' material. And although advice may be given by a consultant, the primary purpose is to enhance the problem-solving capacity of the consultee (i.e. the teacher for the purposes of this study) and merely providing answers to questions is not seen as the most likely means by which this may be accomplished.

According to Conoley and Conoley, consultants aim to provide:

- new knowledge;
- new skills;
- a greater sense of self-efficacy;
- a greater degree of objectivity in the consultee.

West and Idol (1987) make a number of similar points in defining consultation as a technique that always possesses the following six characteristics:

- it is a helping, problem-solving process;
- it occurs between a professional help-giver and help-seeker, the latter having responsibility for the welfare of another person;
- it is a voluntary relationship;
- the help-giver and the help-seeker share in solving the problem;
- the goal is to help solve a current work problem of the help-seeker;
- the help-seeker profits in respect of future problems.

These features may be seen to varying degrees in the three major models of consultation which Conoley and Conoley (1990) delineate as mental health, behavioural, and process consultation.

Mental health consultation, developed by Caplan (1970), is the longest standing approach and was born in mental health rather than educational settings. Caplan conceptualized caregivers' difficulties as growing from either a lack of skills, knowledge, self-esteem, or professional objectivity, with the latter seen as most important. He used the term 'theme interference' to describe the mechanism whereby a consultee's unconscious links with a particular case were capable of causing unusual ineffectiveness. The main purposes of mental health consultation is to reduce theme interference, to help consultees break loose from constricting thoughts or feelings about a particular child. Although these are intrapsychic events, the consultation proceeds through case discussion and problem-solving, thus concentrating upon the relationships between people rather than internal processes *per se.*

Behavioural consultation focuses on consultees only in an instrumental way. It is seen as a more 'straightforward' approach, rather than an attempt to diagnose subtle consultee dynamics. An advantage of this approach is said to be that it provides more specific information about likely time-scales involved and how resistant to intervention specific problems may be. There can be 'entry problems', however, because of the fact that 'behaviour modification' has a bad name in many quarters.

Process consultation, often associated most prominently with Schein (1988), aims to make people more aware of events or processes in their environments and how these affect their work. It recognizes that overt and covert events at work-group level affect outcomes and attempts to improve the staff members' interpersonal skills rather than concern itself with the unconscious dynamics between them. The theoretical origins of process consultation lie in research on small groups, organizational effectiveness and social psychology and an ultimate goal of the approach is to facilitate ongoing organizational review.

Table 7.1   The major characteristics of the three models of consultation

Entry	Strategies	Targets	Evaluation
Model: Mental Health			
Difficult, ambiguous to administrators	Theme interference, build skills, knowledge, increase self-awareness	Primarily consultees	Consultee satisfaction
Model: Behavioural			
Clear processes and goals	Entire range of social learning theory techniques	Primarily clients	Client change
Model: Process			
Increasingly easy due to recent developments in schools	Data collection, feedback, simulation, process analysis, administrator coaching	Interactions among consultees	Climate, morale, productivity

Source: Conoley and Conoley (1990)

Another model of the various theoretical contributions to the practice of consultation in educational settings has been provided by West and Idol (1987). They have attempted to separate out the knowledge base that informs the interaction between the consultant and the consultee from that which provides the techniques and insights used by the consultee with the client (the child in this context). Examples of the latter, deriving from 'Knowledge Base 2', obviously include a range of curriculum and social learning interventions. West and Idol have detected a number of different theoretical domains that have been proposed within the consultation literature as governing the interactions between consultants and consultees (Knowledge Base 1):

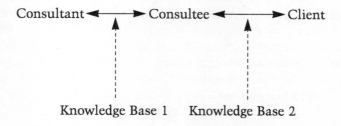

THE DEVELOPMENT OF CONSULTATIVE PRACTICE BY BRITISH EDUCATIONAL PSYCHOLOGISTS

The discussion in Chapters 2 and 3 revealed how the early British advocates of behavioural approaches were soon drawn to considerations of the best ways to create in teachers an interest and enthusiasm for these methods. The writings of Ward, Presland, Leach and others reveal a close concern with such issues as increasing teachers' skills, knowledge, confidence and professional objectivity, although the vocabulary of consultation was not readily available to them at that time. In their problem-solving endeavours, there was a strong commitment to helping teachers generalize these skills to new problem situations as well as encouraging a ripple-like spread between colleagues in schools. Chapters 5 and 6 described how the phenomenon of teacher culture may militate against this process of generalization with respect to management techniques for difficult pupils.

However, whilst some pioneering EPs were directing their endeavours in these directions, others were having misgivings about the whole idea of casework, which tended to be clinically oriented and remote from schools, and were instead turning their attention to the possibility of intervening more effectively with schools by adopting a different starting point. In retrospect, it is possible to see much of this interest as falling at least loosely within the orbit of process consultation. As a growing number of EPs sought to escape from the phenomenon of the waiting list and the unsolicited referral, Taylor (1981) asked what psychological framework would guide EPs in ordering their priorities if they were more able to negotiate their work directly with individual schools. She responded to her own challenge by quoting work in schools that drew to some extent upon the ideas of Caplan and Schein. At the end of the 1980s, Figg and Stoker (1989) also drew on Caplan's model of mental health consultation to provide an account of the management of referrals to an EP service.

Alongside these developments, Burden (1978) had been initiating a series of projects involving trainee EPs working in schools. In the earliest example (Burden, 1974), trainees acted as consultants to teachers in a number of primary schools in respect of pupils with reading difficulties. Breaking away from the individual referral/casework model, these trainees helped the teachers with diagnostic testing and then supported this with lectures and seminars on remedial reading techniques.

Similarly, in the Dart project (Burden, 1978), trainees worked as a group, this time with the pastoral care system in one comprehensive school. A set of guiding principles for this type of work began to crystallize following the Priory project (Burden, 1976) which derived from the request by a newly appointed head of remedial studies in a comprehensive school for help in establishing the most appropriate form of remedial provision. At this stage the two principles of establishing an explicit contract with the school at an early stage in the involvement and of holding regular feedback meetings with all staff involved, rather than just senior personnel or a link person, were established.

Burden's search for an underlying rationale to link together these interventions yielded very few leads within 'the known structures of educational or clinical psychology (although it later transpired that a search through the literature of industrial psychology would have proved far more helpful, viz. Georgiades and Phillimore, 1975; Miller, 1976)' (Burden, 1978, p. 118). A subsequent introduction to systems theory provided what Burden was looking for and the Larches project, in which a primary school in an educational priority area requested help in improving reading standards, was organized and delivered explicitly to incorporate the lessons learned from previous projects within a systems theory framework.

Burden summarized the task for a systems approach in schools as '[to seek] to understand how the explicit and implicit organisational structure of a school affects the perceptions and behaviour of its pupils in a way that leads them to be seen as problematical or disruptive by those faced with the task of maintaining that structure' (Burden, 1981, p. 35).

Miller (1980) drew upon the socio-technical systems theory of Rice (1976) as the rationale for a project in which an educational psychology service directly encouraged all of one LEA's comprehensive schools to become more receptive to a consultative style of work by arranging pairings between senior staff and EPs for visits to other schools, seminars for groups of these senior staff, and the sharing of questionnaire data concerning different schools' priorities for involvement. On a similar theme, in 1977 Hedderley had proposed a model of a psychological service negotiating explicit contracts with schools as to the form and quantity of work it would undertake.

Another strand of practice that was leading towards a similar end was being developed by staff responsible for the EP training course at Southampton University. Cameron and Stratford (1978) originally developed their model of problem selection and management as an experience for trainee EPs in which the latter were each involved in applying the same consistent approach to a different individual referral within one school. The authors then applied the same problem-solving sequence to work with a whole school staff, including dinner supervisors, the educational welfare officer and the school secretary, directed at the issue of managing school-based behaviour (Stratford and Cameron, 1979).

By the early 1980s, a whole variety of in-service provision by EPs for teachers was flourishing. This generally lies outside the present discussion, but in 1982 Cox reported on a week-long in-service course for the entire staff of a Sheffield comprehensive school. A subsequent survey showed an increase in formal and informal contacts between many of the staff. As this involved the whole staff and was process- rather than content-based, it was an intervention geared towards organizational matters within one particular establishment and hence may be construed more as a form of process consultation than was typical of INSET provision at that time. In 1985, Topping provided a broad and selectively detailed review of consultative practice with individual pupils, parents, teachers, and schools as organizations, all in respect of 'disruptive' pupils and with a fairly large proportion of the quoted evidence for effectiveness deriving from the behavioural literature.

Aubrey (1987), in a very thorough review of the literature on consultative practice, emphasized that 'however successful an in-service programme is in changing individual skills, the institution in which the teacher operates has its own norms, role expectations and relationships which form natural barriers to innovative efforts'. Chapters 5 and 6 provide substantiation for this view in the form of the teacher accounts on the effects of school culture. Hence the need for work that also addresses these mechanisms.

One way of making these mechanisms more explicit, including to the staff within the school, and therefore rendering them less obstructive to innovation, is by bringing together staff from different schools to work together on developing strategies for pupils whose names might otherwise fill long referral lists. Although such approaches ostensibly focus upon the needs of particular individuals, they do so in a context where teachers may, through contact with each other, be exposed to new norms and encouraged to develop new expectations of their own and their pupils' abilities to overcome difficulties.

Tempest *et al.* (1987) brought together groups of teachers from 8 to 10 primary schools with an EP and advisory teacher in order to train them in the use of a 'problem clarification model' so that they were subsequently able to support each other in its implementation. The approach was widely disseminated within an LEA and 14 groups were eventually set up, involving 120 schools. Such approaches are characterized by the ongoing nature of the support, whereby the culture of the externally created reference group is allied with the innovation.

Further extensions to, and examples of, consultative practice were provided by early practitioners throughout the decade and in 1990 Stratford gave examples of interventions carried out within infant, junior, secondary and special schools that were all aimed at improving school 'ethos'. Alternatively, others addressed issues of behaviour policy, Leadbetter *et al.* (1992) working directly with a primary school by means of data gathering, feedback to staff and support for subsequent interventions.

In addition to these variations and extensions to process consultation, a smaller number of other workers have provided accounts of interventions with teachers that owe their origins to Caplan's mental health consultation. Hanko (1990) has provided sensitive accounts of groups she has run for teachers, in which it has been possible for them, through discussion of real-life cases, to acknowledge and legitimize their sometimes strong feelings and help each other with possible ways forward. Osborne (1983) has also provided group sessions for teachers to address feelings aroused by the challenge of demanding pupil behaviour, this time drawing explicitly upon a background in psychodynamic theory. Once again, within the general field of mental health consultation, Stringer *et al.* (1992) describe a project in which a group of EPs employed techniques deriving from the Milan school of family therapy for use with whole-school or self-selecting groups of staff.

Given this developing range of influences on the practice of EPs, it is tempting to ask how much, if any, of this has impinged upon those teachers who are the recipients of their services? It is possible, by selectively coding and categorizing areas of the teacher transcripts relating directly to EPs, their advice and their behaviour, to begin to answer questions such as these. However, before this, a brief review will be undertaken of some of the American empirical research into the process and outcome of consultations with teachers of difficult pupils.

EMPIRICAL STUDIES OF CONSULTATION

Whereas the British literature on consultation with schools in respect of pupils displaying difficult behaviour tends to favour case study reports, there are a number of American studies that have undertaken empirical investigations of various aspects of the process and outcomes of consultation.

Research paradigms and consultation

In order to discuss the research in relation to consultation, it is necessary to review very briefly the functionalist and social constructionist philosophical and research traditions, especially in respect of understanding organizational processes.

The *functionalist paradigm* treats organizations as objects that can be subjected to analysis using the concepts and methods of variable-analytic social science. In this view, organizational behaviour consists of objectively observable activities that can be classified, labelled, measured, and related to other phenomena.

Although much of the research into consultation is conducted within this paradigm, Fuchs and Fuchs (1992) have complained that much of what has actually been written about the nature of consultation has tended to concern the consultant/consultee interaction and they quote Gresham and Kendall (1987) who could find *no studies in which researchers systematically assessed and monitored the implementation of consultation plans* by consultees. Fuchs and Fuchs (1992) argued that this issue of treatment integrity did not 'get its due' because it 'went against the grain' with consultants who mainly saw themselves as constructionists.

The *social constructionist paradigm* argues that when consultants intervene in an organization or institutional system, they intervene not so much in the concrete phenomena of power, leadership, decision-making, and structure, but in a system of language constructs, that is, in a system of symbols used by organization members to order and make sense of their experiences. Constructs generally taken by consultants as the target phenomena for intervention are embedded in the socially constructed realities of organizational life. Systems of meaning and interpretation and, hence, the very frameworks for organizational action, are not imposed upon anyone, but are created and sustained in the joint activity of symbolic transaction (Daniels and DeWine, 1991).

Intervention therefore depends on the knowledge and systems of meaning from which organizational members act rather than enforced ideologies or techniques imposed upon the client. Strategic change efforts must create definitions, meanings and interpretations that can be shared widely by organization members. Instead of delivering packaged training programmes, the consultant collaborates with the client in developing a shared meaning of what kind of behaviours will help the organization succeed in its mission and goals.

All the solutions generated are created and maintained with language codes and discourse between the consultant and the consultee. The *consultant and consultee interaction* itself therefore also becomes the model for interaction within the organization, rather than the consultant providing a model for the consultee to imitate and a set of new skills to employ.

As a result of the growing popularity of constructionist perspectives in consultation, Fuchs and Fuchs (1992) have argued that studies have tended to take an adult focus, in West and Idol's (1987) terms, looking far more at 'Knowledge Base 1' rather than focusing on such possible aspects of 'Knowledge Base 2' as 'classroom observation, curriculum-based measurement, applied behaviour analysis, cooperative learning strategies, materials modification, cognitive instruction, and effective teaching' (Fuchs and Fuchs, 1992).

The earlier review of 'consultative practice' by British EPs shows a clear preference for interventions located far more within a constructionist paradigm. The literature from this field concentrates mainly upon interventions concerned with such matters as understanding 'how the explicit and implicit organisation of a school affects the perceptions and behaviour of its pupils in a way that leads them to be seen as problematical' (Burden, 1981). Even when some studies appear to derive more from a functionalist perspective by being focused, for example, upon particular instructional techniques for use with children (e.g. Miller *et al.*, 1985), issues such as creating a mutually supportive culture among participating teachers are usually considered central to the endeavour.

Despite the influence of the social constructionist paradigm upon the practice of many consultants in the USA (and Britain), the bulk of the methodologically rigorous research has been carried out within the functionalist paradigm. Fuchs *et al.* (1992) reviewed 119 articles/chapters and 59 dissertation abstracts published over a 29-year period on consultation *effectiveness*. As a result of the methods used to track down these studies, the authors felt confident that no major pertinent references had been neglected. The main conclusions from this review were:

- Two-thirds of the investigations used group designs as opposed to single case designs (only 'a small handful' of group designs, however, were experimental in nature).
- Behavioural consultation was four times more likely to be investigated than mental health models (50 per cent vs 13 per cent). Organization development (process) models were reported in only 8 per cent, mixed approaches in 7 per cent, with the rest being categorized as 'other'.
- In nearly two-thirds of the studies, teacher or pupil behaviour was used alone or in combination with another criterion to judge effectiveness, whereas pupil achievement was a criterion in only one-quarter of the studies.
- Sixty-five per cent of studies took place in kindergarten to 8th grade classes, only 8 per cent in grades 9 to 12, 8 per cent were in special educational settings and the remaining 20 per cent were mixed.

As a result of these findings, Fuchs *et al.* (1992) argued that to increase knowledge about consultation effectiveness 'researchers must generate new knowledge about which type of situation calls for what type of consultation, and how consultation may be made more effective, efficient, and attractive to teachers'.

The communication process

Bergan and his colleagues (see S. P. Safran, 1991) have conducted extensive research into behavioural consultation in schools. They have looked in particular at the four sequenced steps from applied behavioural analysis with their three associated interviews:

Problem identification: the problem (target) behaviour(s) is/are specified through the Problem Identification Interview (PII)

Problem analysis: the problem is validated and an intervention plan is developed through the Problem Analysis Interview (PAI)

Intervention: the consultee implements the plan.

Problem evaluation: data are analysed to determine whether the desired level of performance has been met through the Problem Evaluation Interview (PEI).

S. P. Safran (1991) has reviewed Bergan's work and drawn out the following as the most significant findings:

- The most important stage of the problem-solving process is problem identification. From a study of 11 psychologists engaged in 806 consultations over individually referred pupils, it was demonstrated that if problem identification occurred, then the likelihood of the intervention being successful increased dramatically (Bergan and Tombari, 1976). This finding is, according to S. P. Safran (1991), frequently cited as the basis for placing primacy on the PII over subsequent interviews (PAI and PEI) in the behavioural consultation process. (It is also probable that this is being recognized, perhaps implicitly, by many of the respondents in chapter 3, who report spending up to a maximum of 90 minutes on negotiating a description of problem behaviour in behavioural terms.)
- From an analysis of the transcripts of 50 Problem Analysis Interviews it was found that elicitative rather than information-giving verbalizations on the part of consultants strongly influenced consultees in identifying resources for a strategy, but not the constraints (Bergan and Neumann, 1980). By 'elicitative' in this context was meant consultant questions aimed at encouraging the consultees to specify what procedures were to be used to implement plans.
- Sixty teachers were given either behavioural information on a child ('elicitors' to verbalize the necessary antecedent and consequent conditions to instruct a pupil), or this plus task analysis, or a medical model condition (information on possible but remote environmental causes and IQ scores) (Bergan *et al.*, 1979). When subsequently observed during a simulated maths lesson, those who had received the

behavioural information plus task analysis, followed by the behavioural condition alone, carried out the most successful teaching. It was also concluded that the medical model information might be detrimental to learning.

The construct validity of the stages of consultation

Tindal *et al.* (1992) have argued that an assumption is often made in the consultation literature that the various stages, especially in behavioural consultation, are discrete events which occur in the prescribed order. In order to examine the construct validity of stages and activities in the consultation process, they trained consultants to use a self-monitoring system and then analysed 10 individual cases in two schools. Tindal and colleagues found the cases 'all to be more different than similar, in the stages they reflected or did not reflect, and in the activities they required'. Problem identification activities appeared sporadically throughout each case; programme planning and development was simply not confined to the middle phases of the process; and evaluation activities often occurred concurrent with data collection (i.e. collecting and using data to ascertain outcomes could not be divided).

Dyadic agreement in consultation and its relationship to outcome

Another new perspective on the conceptualization of, and hence a possibly profitable direction for, consultation research has been provided by Erchul *et al.* (1992). They argued that much of the research into the consultation process, even into the interaction, was obtained from studying one or other party, the consultant or consultee, rather than both. Erchul *et al.* studied 61 consultant/consultee dyads, using a methodology that examined the extent of agreement and disagreement. Most dyads met on 3 to 6 separate occasions (slightly more frequently than reported by the sample of EPs in Chapter 3 – see Figure 3.2) and although the rate of progress through the process varied for each dyad, all passed through recognized stages of collaborative problem-solving. This study showed that the more consultants and consultees agreed upon

- their respective roles;
- the content of the consultation processes (e.g. the extent of teamwork, seeking of clarification, control of the direction of the consultation, consultee resistance to this and objection to specific recommendations);
- the goals for consultation;

then the more positive were consultees' evaluations of:

- consultation outcomes;
- the consultant's effectiveness.

IMPLICATIONS FOR THE PRESENT STUDY

These empirical investigations represent a far more rigorous examination of the processes and outcomes of consultation to schools than are to be found in the British literature. Despite this, however, a number of findings suggest that crucial questions highly relevant to the present study remain unanswered. In particular, the doubt cast by Tindal *et al.* (1992) on the construct validity of the stages and activities of the consultation process suggests that the logically tidy set of stages presented and investigated by Bergan and colleagues does not fully represent its complexity. Although Bergan's stages were present in the consultations, they were far more sporadic and unpredictable than would be implied by a linear model. This suggests that either practitioners pay casual regard to Bergan's model or that the demands of the consultations themselves generate the variability in the different consultations. Given that Bergan's stages are discernible, that is, they are not being completely neglected, it seems more probable that features of the consultations themselves are likely to be responsible for this additional complexity.

These findings suggest that a need still remains for the nature of the consultation process to be more fully explored and mapped. Although structures such as Bergan's model help initially in this, they may also serve the function of advancing study to the point where their simplicity and plausibility are no longer sufficient to account for the levels of complexity they have helped to uncover.

125

Further study of the consultation process is likely to be enhanced by more open methods of investigation that seek to describe the range of variability within the phenomenon under study rather than attempt to fit the complexity of practice into a predetermined structure. If consultants to schools in both Britain and the USA are mainly operating, either explicitly or implicitly, from a constructionist perspective, then this supports the choice of grounded theory as an appropriate methodology with which to investigate this practice.

The next stage in this analysis involves a return to the transcripts of the teacher interviews with a specific focus being placed upon the perceived behaviour of the EPs as consultants. The intention is to weave these transcript data into aspects of the consultation literature in order to elaborate and extend an understanding of consulting to individual teachers who are themselves members of a wider teacher culture.

CONSULTANT CHARACTERISTICS

In order to develop a greater understanding of the role and behaviour of the EP within the temporary overlapping system, the full set of transcripts was analysed again and every comment referring to the EPs' manner, behaviour and suggestions was coded and categorized as before. Four broad categories emerged: knowledge, skills, personal qualities, and aspects of role. The rest of this section will examine these categories in detail in order to focus down on the specific aspects of each that the teachers considered particularly pertinent and to relate these back to the preceding discussion.

The knowledge base

The teachers in this study made frequent reference to the knowledge they assumed their consultant EP possessed. Whilst consultants may aim to impart new knowledge, it is instructive to examine the recipients' perspective in terms of salience and effectiveness.

Many of the teachers felt that the psychologist had had *experience of successful interventions with other pupils*:

She gave some examples of how she'd tried it with other children and they had been very successful. (Interview 11)

She's seen it so many times in so many different places. I mean she's drawing on all her resources isn't she, from previous experiences? (Interview 7)

One teacher also expressed the view that this experience would be much broader than could be gained by a teacher, even one working in a specialist capacity within a school:

It was quite obvious that Cheryl had come across the situation, had lots of information at her fingertips and could actually cheer you up with the news that this child wasn't the worst behaved one in the world. Whereas a member of staff may not have come across the same situation, [even if] they were the special needs expert. (Interview 20)

There was a more mixed view, however, amongst those who commented upon the exact nature of this *specialist knowledge*. A few felt critical that this knowledge did not seem to be any more technical than their own:

I thought perhaps she was looking at it a bit too simplistically. I was expecting something – I don't know how to say it, perhaps a little bit more technical. I didn't expect it to be quite so simple. I think I expected a lot more hype – perhaps something that she would have from her research or whatever. (Interview 18)

The majority, however, saw the knowledge that informed the strategy as characterized by a sense of timing and appropriateness:

He was a professional so he knew what to do ... he was very specific about exactly what I should be doing, the length of time I should be doing it, and so therefore I felt that must be the right thing to do. (Interview 8)

An area of practical knowledge that many of the teachers appreciated seeing in their psychologists was a recognition of the *constraints* imposed upon their time by the realities of classroom teaching. This was a subject that sometimes elicited accounts of other much less successful encounters with psychologists, or stories about the experiences of other teachers they had known:

It was very simple what she did. Because there was no way I could keep reams and reams of notes. (Interview 16)

I think she was very realistic about the programme. I know I have dealt on several occasions with educational psychologists who have

> a rather rosy view sometimes of classroom existence.... I have been
> given tick sheets for how many times they do this or that – quite
> honestly it's impossible to do in a class of that size. There was no
> way I could note down the time they did something or how long
> they did it. (Interview 20)

The main way in which these constraints could be appreciated
was by the psychologist spending some *time actually in the
classroom*:

> He'd been in, he'd watched them, he'd seen me working with them.
> (Interview 3)

> I was quite cross that she was talking about this child on a piece of
> paper, that she hadn't actually got to know Brian and come to work
> with him in the classroom. I can remember going home feeling
> quite angry about that. And that's when I actually asked her if she
> would come in and see him. (Interview 15)

In general, although there are some indications that teachers
perceive psychologists as having a theoretical knowledge base
that may prove helpful, their comments are hedged in with
enough qualifications and reservations to suggest that actual
specialist knowledge *per se* is not seen as the main contributor
to these very successful interventions. Actual examples of interventions that have been devised by the EP and proved successful
were accorded far more credibility. This corresponds with the
finding from Chapter 4 (Table 4.3) that EPs were more than four
times as likely to describe an example from their own experience
as they were to quote more experimentally validated research if
they met with reservations on the part of teachers.

How should this finding be received – as a triumph for pragmatic problem-solving or as a dismissal of the potential benefits
of systematic research?

On the one hand, a social constructionist perspective would
predict that locally contextualized examples would be far more
helpful in creating shared definitions, meanings and interpretations – the precursors for successful consultative work (Daniels
and DeWine, 1991). The strong resentment felt towards EPs
who had not witnessed the pupil in the classroom, however
briefly, also emphasizes the need for a common visual referent as
the basis for discussions. A brief 'snapshot' observation is
acknowledged, almost paradoxically, as not being likely to make
a useful contribution to intervention planning:

It's really just to get them to say 'Yes I can see what you mean' or a bit of – I don't know – it probably wouldn't be any better... I just think it might put a different slant on it. I don't know to be honest, now I've talked about it, it sounds a bit silly. (Interview 14)

However, the contrasting perspective – that the contribution of accumulated knowledge in the form of published research liter-ature is diminished – also enhances the function of the temporary overlapping boundary. The basic tenet of 'scholarship' is that knowledge which exists in researched and published form is potentially available to all. Documented accounts of success-fully managed pupil behaviour provide a greater pressure on schools to make boundary decisions concerning the extent to which they might be able to intervene with difficult pupil behav-iour more successfully and more regularly. By showing support for ostensibly pragmatic approaches, policy changes are avoided and the dependence on the EP as legitimization for altered insti-tutional behaviour is enhanced. The individualistic nature of the EP's 'craft knowledge' as opposed to published technical know-ledge further insulates the procedures of the temporary system from the everyday affairs of the school.

The skills

Three main skill areas emerge from the interviews: listening, questioning and problem-solving, and all are commented upon in far more unequivocal and positive terms than aspects of the knowledge base. *Listening* was seen as an active process, some-times akin to a counselling procedure, that aided problem-solving:

The most valuable thing for us is for somebody to listen to our problems, like talking it through and trying to help us see one thing at a time. (Interview 6)

She listened. Teachers have an awful habit of chipping in, don't they?... She listens and I'm sure she picks up lots of vibes [with parents] just by listening whereas we don't because we're thinking of the answers to the next question. (Interview 15)

Intimately linked up with an active listening approach is the use of *questioning*:

She's had training in listening as well as talking and in the sort of questions she wanted to ask. (Interview 4)

I think the way she questioned me, she got that information and the way she spoke to me, she encouraged me to talk.... I think I almost discovered something of what I was doing myself, and probably I didn't even know I was doing it. (Interview 18)

Both of these skills feed into the *joint problem-solving* that subsequently takes place:

There was that kind of emphasis of looking and exploring ways of developing strategies ... there was sort of a tone of careful step-building ... it was more analytical I think than the way a teacher would handle it and perhaps more objective. Less waffly, perhaps. (Interview 23)

Many of the teachers in the sample commented favourably on the fact that during this planning procedure, the psychologist had *avoided adopting a dogmatic stance*. This point was often made with a sense of relief, as if there had been an expectation of a different type of approach.

She doesn't dictate, she doesn't say 'Do this'. (Interview 7)

I'm delighted to say that I've never been in a situation where I've been told what to do, you know, just like a child. (Interview 6)

I don't think she was trying to teach me my job or whatever. (Interview 13)

Bergan and Neumann's (1980) finding that an 'elicitative' rather than information-giving style on the part of a consultant strongly influenced the extent to which consultees identified resources for a strategy, is implicit in these observations about listening, questioning and joint problem-solving.

Another closely related aspect that emerged from the interviews was that many of the teachers appreciated the working relationship being one in which they could feel at *liberty to challenge* the psychologist's suggestions:

One thing she said that encouraged me was ... 'Some of the things that I'm going to suggest to you will really get up your nose as a teacher.' She said 'I will tell you that now' and she said 'I want you to say ... "it won't work for me".' So that was really good because we had the relationship and I then felt the freedom to say to her 'No, I can't do that.' (Interview 1)

On one occasion I think I just said to him 'It's all right you saying this, that and the other, but it's different when I'm in there and I've got the parents queuing up outside the door complaining.'... We just talked round it, we didn't – we always got on very well. (Interview 17)

The issue of the lack of a dogmatic stance on the part of the EP merits further discussion. The relief surrounding this was fairly widespread and yet it was not based upon previous experience. Only a few of the teachers had had any previous contact with an EP and none of these had been characterized by a dogmatic manner. However, in order for the temporary system to exist in the first instance it needs the presence of a figure, the EP, who has, or is credited with considerable technical expertise or authority deriving from a position of seniority within the LEA.

These attributions, necessary to legitimize participation within the temporary system, lead to a number of the thought processes described by Wagner (1987) as 'knots'. Technical experience is attributed to the EP, but then not valued in comparison to anecdotal examples. An aloof and dictatorial person is expected, and then not experienced. In this way the temporary system is initially legitimized, while sustained participation is subsequently encouraged by personal qualities and aspects of the role of the EP.

Personal qualities

The interviews revealed a complex interaction between what might be termed the personal qualities of the psychologist and the skills already considered above. Although no definite dividing line can be drawn between the two, it is possible to add some clarity to the understanding of successful consultative behaviour by attempting to make finer distinctions.

The most frequently occurring and most widely appreciated of these qualities was the psychologist's *encouraging approach*:

> The first thing she did for me, if nothing else, she made me feel that I was worthy and she made me feel that I was doing the right thing. She made me feel that all was not lost and she gave me more confidence to go on and to persevere ... she was really sort of heartening and she sort of spurred you on to do more. (Interview 18)

Another feature identified by a number of the teachers was the psychologist's *empathy* with the emotional reactions produced in the teacher by the pupil's behaviour:

> He said he would have it all on to cope with these two. I mean he'd been in, he'd watched them, he'd seen me working with them and he said 'It's enough to drive anybody round the bend, you're doing well.' ... Obviously, as a psychologist he was boosting my morale but it's still nice to be told. (Interview 3)

> The feeling that there's somebody else who knows ... If you got so desperate, there's somebody else in the authority who knows what's going on. (Interview 17)

It is debatable whether this encouragement and empathy will in itself lead to these teachers developing a greater sense of self-efficacy (Conoley and Conoley, 1990) in respect of managing difficult pupils. Given the sense of isolation and emotional burden experienced by many of them, as reported in Chapter 6, it is not surprising that these particular consultant qualities were so positively perceived. They may well be necessary steps towards developing a greater sense of self-efficacy but it is unlikely that they are in themselves sufficient.

A slightly different personal quality was the ability to act as a *facilitator of social interactions*, especially in meetings that also involved parents.

> She smiled a lot ... she was just a very calm, collected person. (Interview 16)

> She seemed calm and always positive ... she would never get cross. When we had the small group [of staff] she wouldn't get cross with people and everything she said brought the positive side out of them. (Interview 19)

Aspects of role

In addition to the knowledge and the various skills and qualities that the teachers identified as being important, there was also a range of comments alluding to aspects of the role of the psychologist. Some teachers referred to the psychologist as an *'authority figure'* although the nature of this authority was variously construed:

> He had the authority to make suggestions and he also in a way was taking some of the responsibility. (Interview 3)

> Because it was an outside agency perhaps one feels that you have to respond a little bit more positively to what they are going to be saying. (Interview 22)

By being external to the everyday life of the school, the psychologists were also seen to be more *detached from the emotional effects* of the difficult behaviour. The fourth aim of consultation in Conoley and Conoley's formulation, of course, is to encourage this greater objectivity in the consultees themselves.

He was more detached, he didn't obviously have the same level of panic that I was getting into. (Interview 5)

It's nice to meet and talk to someone who's not involved with the day-to-day turmoil, or can look at it in a detached manner. (Interview 21)

Another characteristic of this more detached position is that it *allows basic information-seeking questions to be asked*. A special educational needs co-ordinator explained how it was far less easy for her to ask the same questions about a pupil of whom she would have at least a fleeting knowledge:

It takes somebody out of the situation. You see if I went in and said to a member of staff, who might be much more mature than me and have a lot more experience .... 'Now what do you mean by badly behaved?', if I said that, it could come over as me saying 'You don't know what badly behaved means' or taken another way. But because it's coming from an objective situation, not having seen the child, and trying to get a clear comprehensive picture, then it's taken in the manner in which it's intended. (Interview 6)

The external position was also seen to contribute to the psychologist being able to act as an *arbiter*, especially between school and parents.

Mum and dad sat over there, Sandra sat there, and I sat there and Miss Jones sat here.... It was an 'us and them' situation. She was very quiet, she listened a lot ... [and] acted as a judge and jury in a way. (Interview 15)

Quite often if you've got an interview between a parent and a teacher, it starts off at an aggressive level.... If an interview is set up with a psychologist, because they are obviously not to blame, there's no element of blame there. It's somebody removed from the situation.... We still get a starting off by accusing the school to a certain extent but then it breaks down and you get to look more into the home side of things because the psychologist is there ... and delves into it. (Interview 24)

Clearly, the issue of being external to an organization or not has direct implications for the work of an internal consultant. These will be returned to in the final chapter of this book. The next chapter, however, turns back to a new section of the transcript data and examines a little more of the phenomenal world inside the temporary overlapping system. It examines in detail the explanatory mechanisms seen by the teachers to account for the difficult behaviour displayed by the pupils in the first place and the reasons for improvements. As parental influences are heavily implicated in these explanations, Chapters 9 and 10 then address more fully the complex question of assigning responsibilities for different aspects of pupils' behaviour at home and school.

PART 3

ASSIGNING RESPONSIBILITIES

CHAPTER 8

Cause and defect? Teachers' attributions for difficult pupil behaviour

> Teachers' ideas about the causes of special needs, particularly learning difficulties and behaviour problems, are likely to affect the attitudes they take towards children with special needs and so too influence the ways in which they react towards them in the classroom. When considering teachers' explanations of the special needs of their pupils it is of interest to set them in the context of the different, and at times competing, explanations available for children's academic failures and behaviour difficulties. (Croll and Moses, 1985, p. 42)

This quote is taken from an account of a survey of 428 junior class teachers carried out in 61 schools across 10 LEAs. As part of their examination of mainstream teachers' knowledge and practice in respect of special educational needs, Croll and Moses asked teachers to give their explanations for the special needs of children in their classes. Causal factors such as 'IQ or ability', 'attitude' and 'concentration' and others were grouped under the general heading of 'within-child', whereas those such as material circumstances at home, parental attitudes or pathological social or emotional conditions, were categorized under 'home'. A summary of Croll and Moses' findings is shown in Table 8.1.

(Teachers were unable to make causal attributions for about one in ten of the children in the total sample, and were also able

Table 8.1   Summary of causal factors

	Behaviour/ emotional problem (N=872)	Discipline problem (N=500)
Any 'within-child' (not including health)	30.8%	38.8%
Home	65.8%	65.6%
Any school/teacher	2.5%	3.8%
Any health/absence	2.6%	1.6%
Any 'within-child' or home factors	80.3%	82.4%

From Croll and Moses (1985)

to select more than one causal factor. Hence the columns do not total 100 per cent.)

The picture to emerge from Croll and Moses' study is a very clear one. Behaviour or discipline problems in children are seen in two-thirds of cases to be due to home factors, in a third to two-fifths to within-child factors, and in only two to four in a hundred cases to any school or teacher factors (including previous schools or teachers).

The present study, although not on the scale of this survey, is able to probe more deeply into the nature of teachers' attributions about the origins of pupils' problem behaviour and is also in the unique position of being able to compare and contrast these with the attributions made for the positive changes that are brought about.

ATTRIBUTIONS OF CAUSALITY, CONTROL AND RESPONSIBILITY

Eiser (1978) has argued that the degree of differentiation within a set of attributions represents the extent of the conceptual elaboration of that set and hence its perceived importance:

> When we make an attribution about another person ... we are essentially trying to interpret or explain his behaviour, and in doing so render our social environment that much more predictable and intelligible. The size of the vocabulary at our disposal is evidence of the importance we attach to doing this.

In addition to the salience of particular attributions, it is especially relevant in the case of difficult pupil behaviour to consider the extent to which attributions of causality are accompanied by an associated sense of responsibility or 'blameworthiness'.

Wiener (1980) identified three major dimensions along which attributions varied: locus (internal or external), stability (transient or stable) and controllability (controllable or uncontrollable). He suggested that affective and behavioural reactions to another's behaviour, as well as expectations for their future behaviour, were influenced by attributions formed on the basis of these three dimensions. His studies showed that whether individuals felt sympathy or disgust for the problems experienced by others and whether they offered help, depended upon whether they saw the behaviour as internal and controllable (e.g. behaviour resulting from drunkenness) or internal and uncontrollable (e.g. behaviour resulting from a disability).

A Canadian study by Johnston *et al.* (1992) examined the causal attributions made by adults for hyperactive and aggressive child behaviours. Young adults were asked to rate various written descriptions of these types of behaviour displayed by 5-year-old and 11-year-old boys. Although they were able to quote previous studies showing that adults often attribute problem child behaviours to causes within the child's control, their study set out to tackle the unanswered question of whether the same result would occur for both hyperactive and aggressive behaviours. Johnston *et al.* summarized their findings thus:

> These results suggest that, although adults perceive hyperactive and aggressive behaviours as equally likely to originate within the child and equally likely to be stable over time, aggressive behaviours are seen as more within the child's control and elicit more negative evaluative reactions. In contrast, adults appear to hold children less responsible for hyperactive behaviours and seem more likely to 'excuse' these behaviours.

Although this study obtained data from 186 young adults, these subjects were drawn from a student population and there has been relatively little by way of empirical investigation of teachers' causal attributions. There have, however, been a number of recent investigations involving parents and Johnston *et al.* quote research linking parents' attributions for children's behaviour to their affective and behavioural responses to that behaviour (e.g. Dix and Grusec, 1985; Dix *et al.*, 1989). Using written vignettes of children's difficult behaviour, Dix and his colleagues found that the misbehaviour of older children was more likely to be attributed to personality factors and seen as intentional than was that of younger children. In addition, if the child was judged to be responsible for, or in control of the behaviour, then parents were much more likely to choose 'power-assertive' methods of discipline. Similarly, Grace *et al.* (1993), in a study involving 115 mothers and 122 adolescents, showed that self-reports of conflict were positively correlated with mothers' and teenagers' attributions of the others' behaviour as being intentional, self-ishly motivated and blameworthy.

Fiske and Taylor (1984) have extended these considerations by presenting an attributional model that includes judgements about the responsibility for effecting a solution to a problem as well as its original cause. This model is demonstrated in Figure 8.1.

Figure 8.1   Fiske and Taylor's model of combinations of attributions for the cause and solution of problems

		Responsibility for solution?	
		Yes	No
Responsibility for cause?	Yes	Moral model	Enlightenment model
	No	Compensatory model	Medical model

Thus, for example, an agent may be perceived as having the responsibility for solving a particular problem whether they were responsible for causing the problem in the first place (moral model) or not (compensatory model). Similarly, differing responsibilities for effecting a solution may also be attributed in instances where an agent is perceived as not implicated in the original cause of the problem.

Related to the study of attribution for difficult pupil behaviour is the area of literature concerned with labelling theory. In British accounts this is usually approached more from an ethnographic perspective and tends to yield more descriptive accounts.

For example, Hargreaves (1975) approached the subject of attribution via the concept of implicit theories. He argued that individuals form implicit theories about what personality traits occur together, deriving these partly from common elements within the culture and partly from various forms of social learning peculiar to the individual. He went on, however, to argue that the attribution of motives or intentions was of greater importance than just personality traits and described how this might take place, concluding that

> once Person has developed a fairly consistent picture of Other he will tend to resist new information which threatens this consistency. (p. 25)

Although the studies reported above have concerned themselves with adults' attributions for children's behaviour, it is, of course, also highly pertinent to consider teachers' attributions for parents. In their ethnographic study of a primary school which drew upon data collected by interview and participant observation, Sharp and Green (1975) set out the processes which such a study would need to examine:

> It would appear that parents should not be studied atomistically but in relationship to other facets of the interactional nexus within the school itself ... it seems important to adopt a dynamic perspective to see how teachers' and parents' typification of each other are generated over time as each attempts to negotiate a meaningful symbolic reality and further their ends in response to the situation they confront. Thus categories of good and bad parents, or good and bad teachers, have to be seen in relationship to the past and present biography of the actors concerned in the ongoing process of their mutual encounters. Similarly, there is a need not merely to look at attitudes but also actions as teachers and parents develop strategies which both derive from and serve to stabilise the complex systems of meaning generated in specific situations. (p. 197)

These studies suggest that a greater insight into teachers' responses to strategies for pupil management may be obtained from an analysis of teachers' attributional processes. They also indicate that certain conflicts and paradoxes may arise in this area. For example, a willingness to feel sympathy and offer help to children displaying difficult behaviour appears to be related to an adult's attribution for the controllability of the behaviour. The studies quoted above, however, have used student or parent subjects. Teachers as professionals, it might be argued, should be expected to make attributions in a more detached manner, but given the high levels of personal distress caused to them by some pupils' behaviour (see Chapter 5), is it reasonable or fair to hold such an expectation? In essence, what is the *professional* attributional response to difficult pupil behaviour, is there any accepted wisdom in this area?

And what of the position of parents? Is it more professional to adopt a moral, compensatory, enlightenment or medical model towards the parents of pupils displaying difficult behaviour? A number of practitioners have provided graphic accounts of the defensiveness and hostility that arises between parents and teachers in these circumstances (see Chapter 9). It is relatively easy for pundits to make bland pronouncements about the value of partnership with parents, but there is an accumulating body of evidence and opinion to suggest that the successes that have been achieved in terms of parent–teacher co-operative efforts on behalf of children with a range of special educational needs may well not translate so readily into work with children who display unsettled and disruptive behaviour in school. It is quite probable that the issues of attribution of controllability and of responsibility for effecting solutions is a major determinant of this state of affairs.

TEACHERS' ATTRIBUTIONS FOR THE ORIGINS OF PROBLEM BEHAVIOUR AND ITS SUCCESSFUL IMPROVEMENT

Within the interviews, specific questions were asked to elicit causal attributions for the origins of the pupils' difficult behaviour and for the improvements that had taken place. The transcripts were also scrutinized for other causal mechanisms included in replies to other questions.

The attribution by teachers of 15 possible mechanisms by which parents may be implicated in the origins of pupils' difficult behaviour, but only 3 by which they may make a contribution to its improvement (Table 8.2), indicates the extent and nature of the detail that has been developed by teachers in accounting for parental influences. Conversely, but not quite so dramatically, there are seen to be 10 possible causal factors on the part of the teachers themselves to account for the origins of

Table 8.2 Teachers' attributions to parents for the origins of the difficult behaviour and its improvement (numbers in brackets refer to the number of cases in which this causal attribution occurred)

Cause	Solution
General management of child (8)	General management of child (3)
Punitive/violent home (7)	Encouragement of child (2)
Absence of father (6)	Feeling supported by teachers (2)
Lack of attention to child (6)	
Divided loyalties re separation/ divorce (5)	
Management of difficult behaviour (4)	
Geographical problems re separation/divorce (1)	
Lack of encouragement (1)	
Atmosphere of disharmony (1)	
Adoption issues (1)	
Parent illness (1)	
Grandparents' influence (1)	
Lack of affection (1)	
House move (1)	
Geographical isolation (1)	

problems and 20 to account for their solution. Again, taking the extent of elaboration as a measure of the complexity of the construction, as suggested by Eiser (1978), these teachers have far more developed accounting mechanisms for their contributions to solving behaviour problems than for their origins or maintenance (Table 8.4). The pupils themselves are attributed with 21 possible factors relating to origins and 13 to solutions (Table 8.3). The extent of these elaborations is summarized in Table 8.5.

Table 8.3 Teachers' attributions to pupils for the origins of the difficult behaviour and its improvement

Cause	Solution
Need for praise (7)	Knowledge of general social norms (6)
Lack of acceptance of social norms (7)	Maturity (5)
'Physical/medical' (7)	Knowledge of specific school rules (5)
Temperament/personality (6)	Feeling valued/self-esteem (5)
Not feeling valued/self-esteem (5)	Respect for teacher (3)
Attention-seeking (4)	Temperament/personality (2)
Lack of acceptance of school rules (4)	Developing self-control (2)
Lack of maturity (4)	Awareness of being monitored (2)
Attention span (4)	Acceptance of school rules (1)
Lack of motivation towards school work (3)	Knowledge of sanctions (1)
Intelligence (2)	Awareness of effect on teacher (1)
Lack of awareness of effect on other children (2)	Intelligence (1)
Lack of knowledge of specific school rules (1)	Awareness of behaviour/reward link (1)
Lack of knowledge of general social norms (1)	
Lack of respect for teacher (1)	
Comprehension level (1)	
Lack of awareness of effect on parent (1)	
'Tough guy' self-image (1)	
'Clutter in head' (1)	
Lack of trust in others (1)	
Effects of bad previous school experience (1)	

Table 8.4 Teachers' attributions to themselves for the origins of the difficult behaviour and its improvement

Cause	Solution
Interest level of work set (4)	Positive attention to pupil (13)
Work expectations/steps set (3)	Interest level of work set (8)
Negative attention to pupil (2)	Work expectations/steps set (5)
Teacher's anxiety (2)	Incentives/tangible rewards (5)
Lack of incentives/tangible rewards (1)	Understanding pupil's personality (3)
Lack of record keeping (1)	Teacher feeling valued (3)
Lack of specific management techniques (1)	Consistent approach (3)
Lack of affection/sympathy for child (1)	Individualized attention to pupil (2)
Teacher not making an exception (1)	Record keeping (2)
Pressure from other parents (1)	Understanding pupil's motivation (2)
	Gaining affection/sympathy for pupil (2)
	Maintaining awareness of pupil (2)
	Having information about home (2)
	Specific management techniques (1)
	Reduction of teacher's anxiety (1)
	Making an exception of pupil (1)
	Pressure from within school (1)
	Didactic teaching (1)
	Prioritizing problems (1)
	Ignoring aspects of pupil's behaviour (1)

Table 8.5   Number of different causal mechanisms attributed to various agents by teachers in respect of the origin and the improvement of difficult behaviours

	Parent	Pupil	Teacher
Mechanisms for origin	15	21	10
Mechanisms for improvement	3	13	20
Origin : improvement ratio	5	1.6	0.5

This table indicates that, in terms of the degree of complexity of the mechanisms implicated in solutions compared to origins, teachers make attributions to themselves that are ten times more favourable than they make to parents and about three times more favourable than they make to pupils. This is the case despite the fact that in 18 of the 24 cases the teachers and parents had directly operated a joint strategy. The phenomenon of observing parents' adherence to one half of such a strategy and yet not crediting those parents with having made a contribution to improving pupils' behaviour is examined in greater detail in subsequent chapters.

Whilst attribution theory would predict the general difference between teachers' attributions towards themselves and others, the difference between the parent and pupil figures requires a different explanation. The extent of elaboration, whilst it may give a strong indication of the relative salience of different factors and categories, cannot give a full picture in terms of attributed *responsibility*. As the dimension of 'controllability' has been shown to be closely related to adults' judgements about appropriate reactions, and the extent of any sympathetic response, to children's behaviours (Dix *et al.*, 1989; Johnston *et al.*, 1992), the data were examined further in this respect.

All the items in Tables 8.2, 8.3 and 8.4 were rated as being of high, medium or low controllability on the part of the agent to whom they had been attributed. Seven trainee EPs also completed the task as an inter-rater reliability check. They were asked to avoid the 'medium' rating if at all possible but were also given a response category of 'impossible to judge'. By pooling these responses with those of the researcher, items which did not receive the same rating from at least six judges were excluded from further analysis. By this means the overall lists were reduced from a total of 81 items to 47, 27 of this latter group being classifed as 'high' in controllability and 20 as 'low'.

The next step was to undertake a case-by-case analysis and note whether high controllability attributions were made within them to parents, pupils or teachers for either the origins or the solutions. Table 8.6 shows the number of interviewees whose high controllability attributions fall into these different categories.

Table 8.6   The number of teachers making *high* controllability attributions to the three agents in respect of the origins of and improvements in pupils' behaviour

	Parent	Pupil	Teacher
Origin	17	9	12
Solution	4	6	21
Origin : solution ratio	4.25	1.5	0.6

This table, by concentrating on causal mechanisms that may be judged to be highly under the control of the agents, offers an analysis that is far more directly linked to teachers' attributions of responsibility. Again parents are seen as being about two-and-a-half times more implicated in the origins of problems, as compared to their solutions, than are pupils. The parents are also seen to be about seven times more implicated than the teachers.

When low controllability mechanisms are considered, the number of teachers attributing these to parents and themselves falls considerably, but rises to a high figure for pupils, as shown in Table 8.7.

Table 8.7   The number of teachers making *low* controllability attributions to the three agents in respect of the origins of and improvements in pupils' behaviour

	Parent	Pupil	Teacher
Origin	3	22	1
Solution	2	14	4
Origin : solution ratio	1.5	1.6	0.25

These figures are not so pertinent to the discussion of responsibility because they represent mechanisms seen as low in controllability and therefore less intentional. It is perhaps not surprising that adults are not very frequently credited with behaving in a manner devoid of intention, but it is interesting to note that many of the teachers see mechanisms relating to pupils, especially in the origins of problems, as beyond the ability of these pupils to alter intentionally.

This leads finally to a closer consideration of the models of responsibility that teachers may incorporate into their attributions in such circumstances. It is possible to analyse the data to ascertain which of Fiske and Taylor's four models of responsibility are involved. From the case by case analysis, it was possible to note, for each agent, whether the conditions for each of Fiske and Taylor's models were present. Examples of some of the combinations are given in the form of quotations to give a brief flavour of the accounts, and then the number of cases displaying each model, arranged against the agent to whom the model applies, is shown in Table 8.8.

Medical model attributed to pupil

Having my own daughter, who is two, I could draw so many parallels between their behaviour. It was incredible because you see he was six and she was two. But he was acting in a very toddlerish way.... It was as if I'd got a big two-year-old in the room all the time....

Well, something worked ... I think he matured obviously as he went on a little bit. (Interview 17)

Compensatory model attributed to teacher

It's nearly always the problem is in the home and your hands are tied a little bit....

I think it was purely and simply because of the total pressure and rules that I kept him under. (Interview 2)

Enlightenment model attributed to parent

The more you learn about his home background the more you realize how negative it is, and has been....

She [mother] needed help in that area of being consistent because she was so extreme. The first sign of anything and he was up to bed for the rest of the evening. It's no wonder he climbed out and wrecked his bedroom because this was tea-time. (Interview 1)

Moral model attributed to teacher

There weren't enough records being kept, and there wasn't enough incentive for him to improve....

I think it was [me] being positive [that led to the improvement] and I think it was the incentive of the rewards. I think it was the attention as well – him having chance to speak to me. (Interview 21)

Table 8.8   The models of responsibility attributed to each agent

	Medical (resp. orig. x) (resp. soln x)	Compensatory (resp. orig. x) (resp. soln ✓)	Enlightenment (resp. orig. ✓) (resp. soln x)	Moral (resp. orig. ✓) (resp. soln ✓)
Parent	6	1	14	3
Pupil	13	3	5	4
Teacher	3	9	0	12

Analysed in this manner, the data yield particularly interesting findings. A chi-squared test applied to Table 8.8 revealed highly statistically significant differences ($p < 0.001$).

By comparing observed with expected frequencies, a compensatory model attributed to the teachers themselves can be seen to have occurred in more than twice as many cases as would be expected. In other words, 37 per cent of this group of teachers adopted a compensatory model, not seeing themselves as having had any involvement in the origin of the problem but still seeing it as their responsibility to effect a solution (and having achieved one). Also, half of the sample adopted a moral model, almost twice the frequency as would be expected, by which they saw themselves as having taken action that had contributed to the problem and assumed a responsibility for enacting (and achieving) a solution.

An enlightenment model was applied to parents far more readily than a moral model. More than half the teachers (58 per cent, again more than twice the expected frequency), although seeing the parents as having contributed to the origin of the problem, did not see the improvement that was achieved as being due to the efforts of the parents. The moral model, which credited parents with a contribution to the solution as well as the origin, consisted of a much lower 12 per cent.

Another model again characterizes the majority of attributions made to the pupils. A medical model in which pupils were seen to have no control over factors responsible for the problem nor to have taken an intentional role in the successful strategy accounted for 54 per cent of the cases, almost twice the expected frequency.

TEACHER ATTRIBUTIONS AND CONSULTATIVE PRACTICE

This form of analysis of the attributions of teachers yields results that differ markedly from those obtained by Croll and Moses (1985). In that study, a far greater proportion of the responsibility for difficult pupil behaviour was located with the pupils themselves, with an even greater share laid at the feet of parents. In the present study, although parents remain predominantly culpable in the teachers' eyes, there is also a greater willingness to explore the possible contributions made by factors within the control of the teachers and their schools. It needs to be borne firmly in mind, however, that these teachers were all chosen because they had experienced successful interventions. In a sample not specifically selected in this manner, results would probably be much more like those obtained by Croll and Moses. The Elton Report did, in fact, detect a prominence for this attributional pattern:

> Our evidence suggests that teachers' picture of parents is generally very negative. Many teachers feel that parents are to blame for much misbehaviour in schools. We consider that, while this picture contains an element of truth, it is distorted. (Elton Report: DES 1989, p. 133)

In subsequent research, it would be extremely interesting to tap into teachers' attributions throughout the course of an intervention rather than in the *post hoc* manner described in this study. Asking teachers retrospectively for their opinions about pupils' previous behaviour and the reasons why change occurred may well elicit different accounts to those from the same types of questions asked prospectively. It may be the case, for example, that teachers are more willing to attribute some of the original causes of a pupil's behaviour to factors within their own control (as in the moral model) once they have experienced a successful outcome deriving from their own actions.

A related issue is that of the attributions likely to surround unsuccessful interventions. Experienced practitioners might speculate that the attribution of highly externalized origins (as in the compensatory and medical models) might be associated with teachers' reluctance to embark upon a recommended intervention in the first place. What might surround a course of action enthusiastically entered upon only to end in disappointment later, would seem far harder to predict.

However, such prospective research might prove extremely difficult to execute. The sample of 24 teachers used in this study was difficult to identify, despite writing a number of letters to EPs in various LEAs. Some informal replies suggested that EPs were concerned that, although they could identify cases where positive outcomes had been achieved, there was an element of fragility about them and continued success was not guaranteed. Even if an adequate-sized sample were to be obtained, the logistical problem of the researcher being present at the occurrence of key moments likely to influence attributions significantly, still remains extremely problematic.

The present study does, nevertheless, yield a number of important findings. Firstly, it provides extensive lists of the attributions used by teachers when confronted by pupil behaviour they find difficult to manage. From within these, the more frequent explanatory mechanisms attributed to pupils are physical or medical factors, a need for praise, a lack of acceptance of social norms and temperament or personality. To parents, general child-management strategies, a punitive or violent home, an absent father and a lack of attention are the most common attributions. Predominant causes attributed by teachers to themselves consist of setting insufficiently interesting work and having unrealistic expectations of the pupil.

The study, especially the analysis in terms of Fiske and Taylor's models of attribution of responsibility, also shows that teachers, even that group who successfully overcome their pupil-management problem, do not all share the same attributional style. However, neither do they possess a random selection. This research has shown, for example, a propensity for teachers to make medical and enlightenment model attributions to pupils and parents respectively, whilst tending to divide themselves between moral and compensatory models.

In terms of implications for practising EPs, this raises the question of how actively they should attempt to alter teachers' attributional styles, if they are of the opinion that these are interfering with the search for an effective intervention. Is it best to ignore such considerations and concentrate on more practical and child-focused considerations from the outset, or is it a vital prerequisite to spend time trying to bring a teacher towards patterns such as those described above, which have been shown to be associated with positive outcomes? If the latter course is chosen, should this be a covert process, or might the seemingly more radical and initially time-consuming option of actually sharing these findings with teachers themselves ultimately lead to longer-lasting positive outcomes for pupils and their teachers?

Despite current professional trends towards a greater interest on the part of EPs in techniques for the management of whole-class groups and in whole-school behaviour policies, legislative demands, in the form of the Code of Practice, still require a considerable amount of attention to be given to the management of individual pupils who are deemed to present management difficulties. In all these styles of professional practice, the attributions teachers make for pupil behaviour are likely in some instances to remain considerable stumbling-blocks to any form of intervention unless they are incorporated more explicitly into the legitimate domains for EPs' enquiries and action.

CHAPTER 9

Home and school: boundaries, barriers or barricades?

How much responsibility for pupils' difficult behaviour should be laid at the doors of parents and teachers? And to what extent should pupils themselves be partly or solely accountable for their own actions?

The answers to persisting questions such as these trip easily from the tongues of those who trade from a distance in polemic and invective but prove frustratingly resistant to resolution for those professionals closest to the issue. Clearly, there are circumstances in which responsibility can readily be attributed in each of the three directions, but equally there are a host of scenarios over which a genuine ambiguity presides. Without careful handling, the legitimate boundary between the respective responsibilities of home and school can grow into barriers of mutual recrimination and even into barricades against any agreed and effective solution.

This chapter will examine the difficulty surrounding this boundary of responsibility and search within the literature of researchers and practitioners for clues to ways in which external consultants can work effectively within this border territory.

BARRIERS TO HOME–SCHOOL CO-OPERATION

The problem of antagonistic relationships between teachers and parents when pupils are experienced as difficult to manage has been graphically described within a range of research studies and accounts of practice. For example, a complex and ambitious British research project carried out by Kolvin *et al.* (1981) provided, amongst its findings, some empirical data concerning the relative effectiveness of certain types of home–school collaboration. Three forms of intervention with 'maladjusted' children attending mainstream schools were contrasted with each other and with a 'no contact' control group. Children from 12 schools were screened using several instruments to identify those with 'neurotic, antisocial, academic and/or peer relationship' difficulties and a group of 270 juniors (aged 7 to 8) and 322 seniors (aged 11 and 12), who became the sample for study, were identified as definitely 'maladjusted'.

One treatment approach was psychodynamic in orientation, whilst a second derived from a behavioural perspective. Of particular interest to our discussion is the third group, which was described as representing the parent counselling–teacher consultation approach. In this approach specially trained social workers provided a service both to parents, in the form of short-term casework aimed at various social, financial and management issues, and to teachers, in the form of consultations over particular pupils. From work with this latter group, the project was made 'dramatically aware' of the 'extreme sensitivities' that can surround attempts to bring together school and home when a pupil is displaying difficult behaviour:

> Attempts were made to lessen mutual distrust and prejudice and ways sought to increase parental interest in the child's education and progress or, more generally, in school activities. Initially, the work consisted of carrying the teachers' ideas to the parents. Occasionally, it was necessary to reassure teachers that parents were concerned and interested.... There was also the far more difficult operation of helping certain teachers to appreciate their personal impact on parents. This was perhaps the most sensitive area the school social workers had to deal with; when it constituted an important issue, it had to be broached with great diplomacy and caution.... Sometimes, before meeting, parents or teachers proposed angry confrontations with each other.... Sometimes the teacher thought the school social worker was siding with the

parents, while the parents thought the opposite. (Kolvin *et al.*, 1981, p. 194)

Similar points were also made in one of the most comprehensive British accounts of a consultative service to schools in respect of pupils exhibiting difficult behaviour. Coulby and Harper (1985) describe and evaluate their work in the former ILEA Division 5 Schools Support Unit – a group of support team teachers, an educational psychologist and a senior educational welfare officer – which provided a service to some 80 primary and 15 secondary schools.

Although there was a recognition that home and family factors would play a part in a pupil's school behaviour, Coulby and Harper were anxious not to minimize the findings from the literature of both school effectiveness, and behavioural psychology: 'the thinking and rationale behind the team and its way of working indicate a preference to locate difficulties of classroom disruption within the school rather than ascribe it to the family of the pupil concerned'. On the other hand, where families were also deemed to require some form of intervention because of additional factors, the team was then able to suggest or arrange for the involvement of another agency.

Coulby and Harper again offered a particularly graphic description of the potential for antagonism between home and school that many researchers and practitioners have noted in these circumstances.

> There is still a tendency in many schools, after a particularly stormy episode, to summon parents to the head's office, in the hope that giving them a tongue-lashing will prove more effective than administering the same to their offspring. In such parental 'interviews' the values of the school and the home can be brought into sharp opposition. The results can range from sullen resentment to mutual blame. Even if the parents are prepared to wave a stick for the school, this can sometimes lead to absenteeism rather than reformation on the part of the pupil. (Coulby and Harper, 1985, p. 14)

Dowling and Taylor (1989) describe outreach work from a clinic to a small number of primary schools. The outreach team consisted of a clinical and an educational psychologist and a teacher from the clinic. The purpose of the project was to attempt to reduce referrals to outside agencies by being available to address difficulties in school at an early stage. They provided a drop-in service for both parents and teachers as separate groups, as well as setting up timetabled meetings for consultations with headteachers and other external support staff.

Once again the delicacy of working between parents and teachers was addressed:

> Often a joint meeting with parents and teachers would seem the logical step to follow the drop-in session. However, careful and skilful handling is required in bringing the two parties together, as the situation can be so polarized that such an attempt could be perceived by the parent as a potential confrontation. The seemingly humble goal of reopening communication between parents and teachers must not be underestimated as it can lead to significant changes in perception of the difficulties and might release the child from the 'go-between' position. (Dowling and Taylor, 1989, p. 26)

Many more examples such as these can be found in the published literature and the informal accounts of those professionals who work between homes and schools. Even where such relationships are of the highest quality, they can be severely tested by difficult pupil behaviour. One reason for this may well be the processes of attribution described in chapter 8. Another, however, may be that parents and teachers actually disagree at times on what constitutes problem behaviour, or on which children are displaying it.

TEACHERS' AND PARENTS' IDENTIFICATION OF PROBLEM BEHAVIOUR

A number of carefully conducted surveys have asked teachers to identify the intensity and frequency of different types of difficult and/or disturbed behaviour among their pupils. These have normally required teachers to complete schedules or checklists specifically devised for this purpose. Some of the studies have also asked parents to complete similar instruments designed to detect problems in the home context. The same finding occurs in each study – that the *majority* of children identified as problems in one setting are not seen as such in the other.

For example, in an Isle of Wight survey of over 2000 children – one of the most thorough studies of childhood problems ever carried out – standardized questionnaires completed by teachers and parents both proved extremely effective in screening out children with psychiatric disorders (Rutter *et al.*, 1970). However, there was surprisingly little overlap between the two sources, with only one child in every six or seven in the deviant group being identified by both parties.

This lack of a close correspondence between teachers' and parents' perceptions of behaviour problems was also demonstrated in the longitudinal study of 343 London children by Tizard *et al.* (1988). At the end of the top infant year, teachers saw 34 per cent of the children as having a mild or definite behaviour problem and parents identified 22 per cent. However, only 30 per cent of those seen by teachers as a problem at school were also seen as problems at home and only 34 per cent of those identified by parents were similarly perceived as difficult by teachers.

This is not just a phenomenon confined to British society; similar results have also been obtained from a study conducted in New Zealand (McGee *et al.*, 1983). This recurring finding suggests that either some forms of behaviour are context-specific in that they are more likely to occur either at home or at school, but not at both, or some forms of behaviour have far more salience for teachers and others for parents. For example, Tizard *et al.* (1988) suggested that some types of behaviour, such as lack of concentration, may be more of a problem in the school setting than at home and that other types, such as fooling around or nervousness and withdrawal, may simply be more likely to occur at school.

The studies have enormous implications for the types of initial discussions that parents and teachers may have when a school is concerned about a pupil's behaviour. Parents may be seen as being 'unwilling to accept that there is a problem', whereas they may genuinely not be experiencing the same difficulties in the home setting. Similarly, parents who mention difficulties with their children at home, when these children are models of conformity at school, may be inaccurately perceived as 'fussing unnecessarily', 'neurotic' or 'incompetent' as parents. The relatively high probability of such judgements being made as a result of differing problem identification on the part of teachers and parents makes the area of attributing causes for difficult pupil behaviour potentially confusing and mutually antagonistic.

Of course, it is not necessary for teachers and parents actually to meet for such attributions to take place. Misconceptions can flourish in the absence of contact and communication. 'It's the ones who never turn up that you really want to see' is a common complaint in many staffrooms and also the title of a chapter by Bridges (1987). This describes the results of a series of interviews in Cambridgeshire with parents who were regular non-attenders at parents' evenings and social events at schools. Rather than mere indifference and apathy, the interviews identified a range of reasons from practical difficulties such as transport, family ties and shift work, through to a concern about not being as confident as some other parents in discussing educational matters. But the most recurring theme in the interviews was a dread of school, often associated with their own childhood experiences, this being most prevalent among those parents who had minimal or no contact.

It is not hard to imagine such a parent avoiding contact with the school, however welcoming the invitation. If the situation arises when the school wishes to discuss any matter, especially behaviour, it is also not hard to imagine this parent's manner, fuelled by adrenalin and defensiveness, coming across as 'aggressive' or 'belligerent' or, at the very least, 'unco-operative'.

DEVELOPING A COMPREHENSIVE MODEL OF PARENT–TEACHER CONSULTATION

We now turn our attention to what is known about successful work with teachers and parents when a pupil is displaying difficult behaviour in school. Because of the extreme sensitivities that can surround this area of work, a consultant working without a clear framework runs the risk of exacerbating an already tense situation and escalating a barrier into a barricade.

Fortunately, such a framework can be derived by modifying West and Idol's (1987) model from Chapter 7. In this formulation, Theory 1 is concerned not just with how the consultant works with the consultee – the teacher – but how the consultant works with both the teacher and the parent and, particularly, the relationship between them. Theory 2, as before, refers to the theory behind the strategy employed with the child, but this

Figure 9.1 The two theoretical frameworks that guide consultations with both teachers and parents

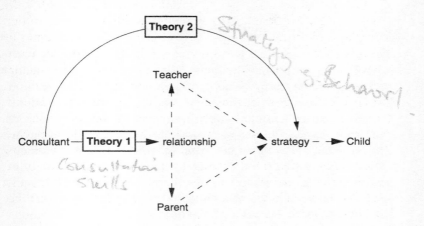

time the strategy often involves both the teacher and parent working with the child.

We shall now consider in some detail the development of approaches from which Theory 1 can draw and the behavioural strategies involving both home and school which are able to inform Theory 2.

Various terms, such as eco-structural (Aponte, 1976), joint systems (Dowling and Taylor, 1994) and ecosystemic (Cooper and Upton, 1990), are used to refer to consultative approaches that consider the interactional aspects of parent and teacher functioning. As such, publications in this area tend to be in the form of theoretical formulations or model building, sometimes backed up by one or two case studies.

Although also concerned with how a consultant works with teachers and parents to effect changes in a child's behaviour, these publications differ considerably in their focus and style from studies of behavioural approaches. For instance, there is very little attempt to collect quantitative data, and outcomes are usually judged in a very impressionistic fashion. Secondly, the role of the consultant and the interaction patterns involved are usually seen as highly pertinent, whereas these are barely mentioned in the behavioural literature. Not only are they seen as important, it is often the case that the relationship between

159

home and school has deteriorated so badly that its *repair* is seen as the major task in itself.

Joint consultation with teachers and parents

The earliest reference in the literature to dealing jointly with schools and families in instances when children are showing unsettled or disturbing behaviour is to be found in Tucker and Dyson (1976). These professionals were, respectively, a family therapist and educational consultant with a family psychiatry department and a senior administrator for a school district in Pennsylvania. They described a pilot project with two elementary schools, the purpose of which was to test the feasibility of utilizing the processes of family therapy to reverse the maladaptive school behaviour of children and facilitate constructive interactions both between the school and home, and among school personnel. They were concerned that parents and teachers seldom met outside formalized contact times unless there was a severe problem, and that under such circumstances these meetings became a confrontation between adversaries in an atmosphere of 'alienation, scapegoating and blame'.

A major intention was to diminish this mutual scapegoating by helping parents and teachers understand each other's motives and actions. One major method used was a series of weekly meetings involving three or four teachers who taught the same children, the principal, the school psychologist, and the family therapist. It was reported that, in these discussions, teachers frequently gained greater insights into the ways in which they might be encouraging some of their pupils' provocative behaviour. Tucker and Dyson commented that as the group proceeded it became apparent that it was functioning in ways frequently observed in families, with the teachers often acting as a group of siblings.

In a later stage of the project, families of children who were having difficulties in school were invited to meet with the principal, the psychologist, a member of the teaching team and the family consultant. By using principles deriving from family therapy practice – the definition and observation of boundaries, clarifying roles, creating a non-critical atmosphere – the authors claimed to be able to provide the security that permitted and encouraged individuals to share relevant material within agreed parameters. Some of these meetings were held with the expectation that a family would accept a referral for family therapy, but many were intended solely to serve the purpose of exchanging information, modifying perceptions, and sharing ideas and suggestions. Tucker and Dyson claimed that the project produced substantial benefits for the schools, the families and the body of professional knowledge.

Following this work, Aponte (1976), also working in Pennsylvania, laid down some of the theoretical basis for what he called 'the ecosystemic or structural approach':

> One must conceptualise the child, the family, the school, and the community organisation involved in the child's problem as systems – interrelated in an ecological complex over a common issue. Their relationships make up the underpinnings of the context, namely its structure. The transactional patterns that characterise the relationship among the component systems of this complex incorporate the laws by which the parts of these systems function with respect to one another.

Aponte illustrated the approach in action with a case study of a 10-year-old who was frequently involved in fights with other boys at school. In this example the therapist – the intervention was being carried out from a Child Guidance Centre base – brought together for an initial meeting in school two therapists, the three teachers who taught the pupil, the principal, mother, father and child (they had wanted to include the five siblings as well!). Important role implications for the therapist, consultant or whoever is responsible for the intervention are pointed out:

> The teachers ... do not expect to be treated as clients. The prospect of being interviewed with the child and his parents brings into question the school staff's status in relation to their pupil. And yet the therapists are being called upon to accomplish something neither the family nor the school could do and thus [they] must lead the three-way effort ... to solve the problem.

Taylor (1982) discussed family consultation carried out in school settings by an educational psychologist. She saw a significant difference between this 'school-based family consultation' and the regular practice of family therapy in that the educational psychologist would be working within a particular school with both the staff and the pupil population for a number of years. 'He can therefore use a different time-scale and especially he can influence the school system to support his interventions once he has seen the family.' Taylor described the responsibility placed upon a pupil to act as 'go-between' when the two systems of family and school fail to mesh: 'As the lynch-pin between them he is the focus of the greatest stress and any indications of a bad fit are going to manifest themselves in him.'

Using two case studies, Taylor outlined a method of working which involves an initial family interview in school followed by continuing consultations with school staff. In one case study, she described involving two of the school staff for the first half-an-hour of the family consultation 'to voice the complaints of the school and to have an initial response from the parents and [the pupil]'. This understandably generated strong feelings in the parents and these then became the focus for much of the rest of the meeting. In this way Taylor was working to some degree along the lines described by Aponte but had pulled back from a full application of his ecosystemic approach. Aponte acknowledged the difficulties as well as the benefits posed by working with members of the two systems always physically together and Taylor opted for some separation between the two.

Taylor saw the theoretical roots of this type of practice as lying within a number of fields.

> The would-be consultant ... owes a debt to many approaches in the field of mental health ... a psychodynamic understanding of the life cycle; systems theory, learning theory and crisis theory; techniques of brief therapy, family therapy and consultation; and, for work in schools, at least a nodding acquaintance with the literature of organizational development. Trying to determine which is the major influence in this or that tactic can lead to the proverbial problem of the centipede.

In other words, interventions are not chosen by a strict application of a particular body of theory; rather, 'parameters and techniques' that derive from these backgrounds are employed. These include taking the presenting problem seriously, defining it in practical terms and sometimes 'reframing' it. An emphasis is placed upon tasks:

> It is imperative to find early in the interview an explicit focus to work on which is accepted by the family and has meaning for them.... Tasks which involve the school and the family can help to change the dysfunctional interaction between the two systems and can be regularly monitored by the consultant on his regular visits to school.

In 1983, Fine and Holt again reviewed the approach advanced by Tucker, Dyson and Aponte, and illustrated a well-written article with further case studies. They suggested that although such an approach might lead to interventions similar to those deriving from other perspectives, the systemic approach involved participants in a broader form of analysis and planning:

> The teacher may end up using some reinforcement or encouragement strategy or some restructuring of academic tasks. These 'traditional' techniques emerge, however, from a broader, systemic view of the child.

In concluding the article Fine and Holt drew on their experience of this type of work and cautioned other practitioners against unrealistic expectations by highlighting five important considerations.

They drew attention to the sophisticated and dynamic nature of consultation with a systems orientation. It was far harder to draw up a set of repeatable procedures for a consultant, they argued, than it was in the use of behavioural approaches where standard formats and manuals were in existence. Because of this, some consultants felt less comfortable, by virtue of their own temperament, with work with a far less predictable course of action and outcomes. Problems with identification of the 'client system' were also raised. Within a more traditional mental health consultation position, 'the client, that is, the child with a problem, is seen as the responsibility of the consultee, the teacher. . . . When the consultant views the client system as the child in interaction with the teacher and the classroom environment, then the consultative relationship is likely to change.' The homeostatic nature of organizations such as schools was also raised, in the sense that if a consultant had already been typecast as, for example, a child counsellor or tester, then there might be resistance to an attempt to change roles to a systems level consultant. Finally, Fine and Holt temper their own enthusiasm by pointing to the *absence of data-based research* to support the efficacy of a systems approach within schools.

In 1985, Dowling and Osborne's book (revised in 1994), *The Family and the School: A Joint Systems Approach*, brought together a collection of papers by practitioners associated with the Tavistock Clinic. In the opening chapter Dowling set out the theoretical framework for the 'joint systems' approach, adding to earlier formulations which drew mainly upon concepts from family therapy by drawing parallels with the systems thinking developing in relation to educational institutions. In particular, she points to notions such as decision-making executive sub-systems within both family and school systems and to the prominence and nature of rules both in the form of ground rules and meta rules, the former referring to the specifics of the way a system functions and the latter to the meaning of the ground rules.

At the same time, in the American context, Power and Bartholomew (1985) presented in some detail a case study aimed at intervening between a school and family system, 'getting uncaught in the middle' as they termed it. These workers, a psychologist and a consultant, drew upon the family systems approach of Minuchin and Haley to provide a model for their intervention planning with a 10-year-old boy whose teachers were concerned about his poor academic performance and his facial tics. This paper went further than the earlier examples of ecosystemic approaches by providing a more detailed assessment of the problem in terms of symmetrical relationships and hier-archical problems, and joint meetings with staff and parents were planned and conducted in the same way as family therapy sessions.

In this particular case the home–school conflict was seen as providing an issue on which the parents could collaborate and thus afford a partial solution to their own relationship problems.

> To become 'uncaught' the team needed to understand how the family–school pattern mirrored the family pattern, establish a clear boundary between the home and school domains, validate the authority of each party in their own domain, and provide a new way for the parents to unite their energies.

In addition to recognizing the need to work with this dynamic, Power and Bartholomew also acknowledged 'a dilemma common to school consultants':

> Since the team was contracted by school personnel, in effect they were mandated to validate the school's position in the conflict. If the team had not sanctioned the school's position, any power they had as consultants would have been lost.

Notions of the client and lines of accountability thus intervene directly to determine the types of strategy that are acceptable to some or all of the parties concerned, *early acceptability* being the *sine qua non* for any successful action.

Returning to the British context, Campion (1984) described her use of a family therapy approach as an educational psychologist. Clinic-based sessions were organized for families where children had been referred for various school-based problems deemed by the author to have their origins within the family background. She does not detail the form of work undertaken with the schools but states that for many of them a 'joint systems' approach was attempted, with an intervention at school 'which would complement the intervention in the family system'. The account discusses the nature of the family problems and various features of the therapeutic interventions, the majority of which comprised 5 to 8 sessions with some or all family members attending. Of the 72 children worked with, Campion's evaluation, based on reports from school, showed that 42 had made more satisfactory progress and the main reason for referral had disappeared, 27 had made a partial improvement and 3 had shown little or no improvement.

Subsequently, Cooper and Upton (1991) published a series of articles extolling the benefits of the ecosystemic approach as a new method for conceptualizing behaviour problems which 'opens up exciting new avenues for intervention'. They argue that these approaches, using interventions such as 'reframing and positive connotation', are in many cases suitable for autonomous use by teachers without the need for expert supervision. Although they recognize the value of consultancy, Upton and Cooper (1990) believe that there are many situations in schools in which these techniques could be used independently by teachers or within the context of peer support groups. In view of the intensity of reactions between parents and teachers and the strength of the attributions often made when a pupil is perceived as displaying problem behaviour, it is difficult to imagine teachers frequently reframing the problem entirely of their own volition, and the need for consultant or possibly peer intervention may have been underestimated by Upton and Cooper.

The preceding accounts all display a deep concern with the dynamic relationships between teachers, parents and outside consultants. Although Taylor (1982) and Fine and Holt (1983) refer to the importance of tasks that can be understood by both parents and teachers and carried out by one party or both, the selection of the tasks themselves is not presented as being particularly problematic. The final part of this chapter turns its attention to those sections of the behavioural literature that focus specifically upon task-based strategies that involve both teachers and parents.

Behavioural approaches with teachers and parents

Traditional behaviour modification approaches in classrooms can, as has been shown in Part 1, take up a great deal of time and effort on the part of teachers and consultants. Often the teacher must alter his or her teaching style, and tangible rewards are limited or alien within the classroom. On the other hand, parents often have access to a wide variety of privileges. In home-based reinforcement (H-BR) studies, the teacher is responsible for specifying the classroom rules, determining rule violations and communicating these to the parent. At home the parent is responsible for consistently dispensing rewards and sanctions to the child, based on the teacher's report.

Atkeson and Forehand (1979) reviewed 21 papers that contained the results of 29 experiments or case studies using H-BR to influence the conduct or academic behaviour of pupils across the statutory school range. This review also scrutinized the methodology of these studies in order to evaluate the validity of the results and concluded that 63 per cent had 'adequate designs', predominantly ABA designs with one experimental–control group comparison. The general conclusion from the paper was that H-BR was consistently effective in improving both academic achievement and disruptive classroom behaviour across a wide range of ages, in both ordinary and special classrooms.

In the same year Barth also reviewed this subject and considered 18 of the studies included in Atkeson and Forehand's paper. However, by taking a different emphasis, the two papers serve a useful complementary function, especially as Barth discusses a number of the more elusive 'implementation' issues. For example, he quotes a study by Karraker (1972) in which three methods for training parents in the use of H-BR were compared.

One group was instructed in two one-hour sessions with the consultant, a second group had only one 15-minute session with the consultant, while the third group were mailed a one-page instruction sheet. It was found that the method of instruction was not predictive of the amount of behaviour change. Whilst this study goes some way beyond the usual concerns of experimental approaches, it still gives no insights into the actual recruitment of the groups, their expectations and the 'micropolitical' contexts within which the child's behaviour is being experienced.

Again in the area of implementation, Barth quotes from Hickey *et al.* (1977) who examined whether or not home–school programmes actually increased parent–teacher communication. They concluded that such interventions definitely did; in a programme involving 5 children and their parents no instances of parent-initiated contact were recorded during the baseline period but 20 such contacts were observed during the parent involvement stage.

A third study quoted by Barth, that by MacDonald *et al.* (1970), raises interesting questions related to the monitoring of such interventions. In a programme involving 35 adolescents who were school phobic, two groups were randomly assigned to either a 'contact counsellor' or a 'contingency counsellor'. The contact counsellors made three times the amount of parent contact as the contingency counsellors, but the latter utilized daily notes home, with the result of significantly improved attendance for this latter group.

In conclusion, Barth was as enthusiastic about H-BR as Atkeson and Forehand, and stated that 'the wide-scale application of this system need wait no longer'. Despite such reviews and recommendations, however, the approach has not generated widespread discussion in the British literature, although chapter 3 found the inclusion of parents to be a common component within behavioural interventions devised by EPs and primary school teachers.

Leach and Byrne (1986) carried out a successful H-BR study in an Australian secondary school with 4 disruptive pupils and extended their design to see whether any 'spill-over' effects could be observed in terms of improvement in the behaviour of non-targeted but equally disruptive pupils in the same class.

Such effects were indeed observed in one class but not in the other and the authors speculate on the possible reasons for this. Leach and Ralph (1986) provided a case study in an Australian setting which was successful in decreasing the classroom rule violations of a 16-year-old boy, and Gupta *et al.* (1990) have reported on what they consider to be 'the only study which has been carried out in the UK which has attempted to assess the effectiveness of H-BR'. From a study of 24 children selected from two 'bottom-stream' Year 9 classes, Gupta *et al.* were able to claim that 'on the whole the implementation of H-BR improved these children's behaviour, attendance, motivation and the amount of work completed'. It should be noted, however, that this AB design would not fall within Atkeson and Forehand's criteria for acceptable methodology.

An account of a service application of home-based reinforcement in a British context has been provided by Long (1988). He described the work of EPs and behaviour support teachers in West Norfolk and the process of moving away from a system of off-site units for pupils with severe behaviour problems and towards supported home–school links. The focus in this work was placed upon the outside support professional taking responsibility for setting up and monitoring the home–school programme.

The approach used drew upon Topping's (1983) review of provision for disruptive adolescents and the effective elements of the system were seen as being the use of a 'behavioural, problem-solving approach, an emphasis upon the primacy of home–school liaison and ... an effective home–pupil–school communication system'. Long recognized, as have most writers on this subject since Aponte, that a person outside both the home and school system 'can offer support, advice and apply pressure when necessary' in interventions that may well involve both home and school significantly changing their perspectives on the nature of the 'problem' and their respective responsibilities.

The particular tasks for the outside professional in this system were:

- To set up the school–parent interview. Long considered it important that this meeting was held at school because the precipitating events had occurred there and it might therefore be easier to air and clear up any early differences between home and school in the latter setting. The consultant also outlined the options available both in terms of the possible routes such as suspension, special education or home tuition, and the negative aspects of these, and in terms of the success rates of the recommended home–school report system. If the parents wished to be involved with the report system their suggestions regarding such aspects as possible home-based reinforcers were then used in the joint planning of the reporting system.

- The second task for the support worker was to visit home and school to ensure that the report was being implemented and to back up parental management. In the initial stages these visits were made at least weekly.
- The final phase for which the support worker took responsibility was the running down of the system. This was achieved by decreasing the frequency of reporting and visits when all agreed it to be desirable.

Long has evaluated the outcome for 44 cases treated in this way. These pupils were worked with during an academic year by 2 support workers covering a secondary school population of 4,700, and they represent that 1 per cent or so whose problems had previously proved chronic and intransigent. Using Topping's finding of a 66 per cent 'spontaneous remission rate' as a comparison, the West Norfolk intervention achieved an 82 per cent success or partial success rate. Full success (64 per cent) was defined as immediate improvements in attendance and behaviour at school as ascertained by a post-intervention school questionnaire, and partial success as attendance with a barely tolerable (but improved) level of behaviour.

Within the behavioural paradigm, another small but relevant set of literature is concerned with the possible generalization of the effects of a behavioural intervention carried out in a particular setting. This interest followed from the work of psychologists who had achieved considerable success in teaching parents to use behavioural approaches in order to manage their children's difficult behaviour at home (O'Dell, 1974). Two papers describe experimental approaches to determine whether a successful 'parent behaviour training program', one which leads to a child's improved behaviour at home, will generalize so that positive changes also occur in the child's behaviour at school.

Forehand *et al.* (1979) worked with 8 mother-and-child pairs, the children being aged between 5 and 7 years. A control child of the same age and from the same class was also observed. Data were collected by independent observers before and after treatment in the home for the experimental group, and in each child's school for both the experimental and control group. In the home of the treated children both parent and child behaviours changed in a positive direction but no significant change occurred in the school behaviour of either group of children. Reviewing this study and others, McMahon and Davies (1980) concluded that

> If the child is a behaviour problem in the classroom, then it appears that parent training is not the treatment of choice (except, of course, for the remediation of any concurrent home behaviour problems). Instead, appropriate classroom management strategies should be implemented.

No genera-lisation

The small body of literature on 'reward preference' studies, although it does not report directly on interventions, has a very direct bearing upon this discussion in that it has the potential to make a particularly significant contribution to approaches deriving from a behavioural perspective. Caffyn (1987, 1989) surveyed 510 pupils and 99 teachers from four mixed comprehensive schools to gather their views about the effectiveness of commonly used rewards and punishments. This study asked questions about both school work and behaviour. In both categories, and for both pupils and teachers, involving parents was seen as of fundamental importance.

A similar study was carried out by Harrop and Williams (1992) with junior-aged pupils and their teachers. The pupils and teachers of Years 5 and 6 in two primary schools (a total of 84 boys, 97 girls and 8 teachers) each ranked 10 rewards and punishments for effectiveness. The pupils were asked to rank these according to how much they would help them 'work better in school' and the teachers according to which were the 'most useful'. The pupils rated their parents being informed about their good and naughty behaviour as respectively the most effective reward and punishment. Although informing parents about naughty behaviour rated second in the teachers' punishments (after 'being told off in front of the class'), informing them about good behaviour came eighth on their list of rewards. Harrop and

Williams describe this as a 'gross discrepancy' that 'suggests a rather negative attitude which requires examination'. Clearly, when pupils' views are solicited concerning the significance of contact with their parents over school work and behaviour, they consistently see this as highly important.

Combining ecosystemic and behavioural approaches

The areas of literature reviewed in this chapter under the headings of 'ecosystemic' and 'behavioural' approaches may be contrasted in many ways. For example, the former is more discursive whereas the latter attempts to remain firmly based upon quantifiable data. They also draw upon very different, and sometimes antagonistic, theoretical perspectives.

Both of these perspectives, however, have a clear contribution to make to the extended version of West and Idol's consultation model shown in Figure 9.1. Ecosystemic and related processes provide the consultant with a model (Theory 1) to guide the way he or she works with the teacher and parent relationship so that barriers are overcome and positive attributions are encouraged. Another set of principles from the behavioural literature (Theory 2) is able to inform the joint strategies that are devised in order to help in the management of the child.

Obviously, the literature on behavioural approaches has traditionally concerned itself with Theory 2. Although early British writers like Presland (1975), Ward (1976) and Leach (1981) talked about the need also to address the consultative aspects of working with schools, there was little in their writings or that of their contemporaries that reflected anything like a systematically developed body of theory (Theory 1) with which to describe, co-ordinate and possibly even predict aspects of this part of the work. Conoley and Conoley (1990) have pointed out that still 'in contrast to mental health consultation, there is limited literature concerning relationship issues between the consultant and consultee' in behavioural approaches.

The studies described under the heading of ecosystemic approaches focus far more on this relationship and the interactions between school staff, parents and the consultant and thus offer frameworks that might inform the development of Theory 1, as the transcripts are coded further in the next chapter.

CHAPTER 10

Home and school: locating the boundaries of responsibility

Practitioners would argue that relationships with parents, which always have the potential to become confrontational or at least discordant, are usually never more stretched than in the case of difficult pupil behaviour. Where does the responsibility for taking action begin and end for the school? How is the behaviour to be explained and what causal attributions will be made? Who decides on the terminology and the hypothetical mechanisms to be invoked in any attempted explanation, whether or not these are articulated?

IDENTIFYING AND SURMOUNTING BARRIERS

Throughout the interviews the issue of an original 'lack of support' or 'back up' from home was cited. The teachers perceived it to be impossible to feel a unity of purpose and action with parents over the difficult classroom behaviour of their children; a barrier was perceived and attributed to the parents:

What we lacked before was co-operation from the parents. (Interview 20)

We did try to get the parents involved. We got very little support from home at that time. (Interview 22)

In open systems theory terms, these perceived barriers may be construed as 'boundary issues' between school and home. The interviews reveal four different aspects of these: the system's internal functioning; the negotiation of shared meanings across the boundary with the environment; uncertainty over the predictability of aspects of the environment; and uncertainty over the actual location of the boundary itself (Rice, 1976).

Internal functioning

Maintenance functions within a system enable its members to contribute towards the primary task rather than having to divert their energies unnecessarily into preserving homeostasis. These maintenance functions take the form of administrative procedures and a common identification with a set of beliefs, values and norms.

In the interviews, administrative procedures were not seen as a barrier to working with parents, except in one case where the teacher said,

> To be honest, I didn't actually see a great deal of the parents, they usually went straight to the head. (Interview 22).

More significant was the teacher's obligation to share the responsibility for the way the school had previously responded to the child or parent, either in terms of being unable to acknowledge the possible legitimacy of a parent's claim or by being the recipient of angry feelings originally engendered in respect of another member of staff.

> [Mother] was very critical of how he'd been handled in the past.... You have to handle her very carefully in a certain manner. I think in previous years that hadn't been done. (Interview 18)

> [Mother] was very anti Miss Roberts [headteacher]. (Interview 15)

The negotiation of shared meanings

In order to function, an institution must arrive at shared definitions of problematic situations. Particularly in the case of difficult behaviour, where the sense of individual threat to teachers' professional competence is so high, it becomes imperative to have an explanatory framework that will command collegiate acceptance. However, such definitions are often unacceptable to parents and apprehension or uncomfortable experiences in this area form a frequently cited barrier to working with parents.

> His mother said he never misbehaved in the home and that was the biggest stumbling block because he was 'good at home' and she was blaming the school. (Interview 2)

> She was very protective of Gary, in her eyes he can do no wrong. (Interview 22)

> I didn't think the mum thought he was a problem. (Interview 14)

Such definitions, which evidence does or does not require attention, the actual descriptors used, and the explanatory mechanisms to be assumed, implied or elaborated – all these are derived during a process of socialization into an institution. To members of the institution they become part of the shared, taken-for-granted, commonsense knowledge (Berger and Luckman, 1966). However, parents, in addition to having different perspectives and interests, are also not party to this institutionalizing process. It is little wonder therefore that attempts to include parents within the teacher's or school's definition by means of a few, or even one meeting, lead to such angry exchanges:

> Mother is very, very nervous and flares up at the slightest thing. (Interview 18)

> [The parents] were very very touchy. (Interview 23)

> Mother had caused so many problems here. She's a very bristly lady. (Interview 15)

> The mother had come in and had a row with the supply teacher in front of the whole class ... shouting and screaming at her. (Interview 7)

In these examples the emotional interactions are all attributed to characteristics of the parents, usually 'the mother'. However, although less common, there was also some recognition that a barrier to communicating effectively might also originate from the school's side, in the form of a lack of certain interactional skills. These are sometimes alluded to during answers to questions about the particular abilities that seem to be possessed by the EP:

> Maybe we didn't talk as straight as Tina (EP) would have wanted us to. I know she goes into the homes and seems to have a good rapport ... but I think perhaps we flannelled a bit. (Interview 7)

She's (EP) had training in listening as well as talking and in also the sort of questions she wanted to ask. (Interview 4)

Interestingly, in these latter examples the differences that the teachers see between themselves and the EPs are in terms of interactional skills, whereas the parents were all construed in typifications concerning emotional instability. In considering the parents, the psychologists and themselves, no teachers construed the interactions as reflecting the various role positions of each party with respect to the other.

Uncertainty over the predictability of aspects of the environment

In systems theory, uncertainty in the environment, the inability to predict the nature of interactions across the boundary because of the possible range of behaviour that may be encountered in sections of the external world, is taken to be a major contributor to decreasing homeostasis of the system. Working with the parents of pupils exhibiting difficult behaviour provides ample scope for such uncertainty and examples have already been provided of this in the construction of parents as emotionally unstable.

Another major aspect is a teacher perception of parents having an alien lifestyle or set of mores. Although this aspect is often linked to a possible explanatory mechanism for a pupil's behaviour, there is also a sense that it exists in some teachers' eyes as a barrier to working together:

He's got no dad but there's a man living there. (Interview 14)

She [mother] has a series of boyfriends ... she talks about different men being there. (Interview 9)

She watches adult films and has a lot of adult vocabulary on occasions. (Interview 20)

The uncertain status of a parent's (always the mother's) sexual relationships is often referred to as though it automatically makes conversation or problem-solving more contentious. Other teachers in the sample, however, also make very favourable comments about the effects of a new partner on the pupil under discussion.

A final source of the perceived barrier derives from judgements about the intellectual ability or maturity of a parent.

175

assuaging

[Mother's] really like a girl of about 14 ... not very bright but she means well. (Interview 3)

Uncertainty over the location of the boundary with the environment

Another common uncertainty concerns the degree to which parents and teachers might construe differently the extent of each other's responsibilities and thus lead to difficult boundary transactions – in fact, to a difficulty in deciding upon the exact location of the boundary itself. Teachers sometimes expressed a lack of confidence about the extent to which they would or should be allowed to enquire about events at home and offer advice and suggestions:

I think sometimes they think 'Oh you're prying'.... Because (EP) is involved, somebody official, it's not so much like prying, it's not like prying from school. (Interview 9)

The mother came in looking for assistance originally and said 'Smack her if she needs it – she needs a good wallop sometimes'. But to me some attention from the mother would have gone a long way to assuaging some of the difficulties we were having with the child. (Interview 20)

I wouldn't like to start involving parents with things like money if I didn't know it was going to be profitable(!). (Interview 11)

I don't remember us actually saying 'Look, he needs a wash!' (Interview 7)

There is also a belief that the home culture is such that any comments from school about a pupil's behaviour will only contribute to a downwards spiral for the child or parent or both:

I'll say to her sometimes 'What's he been like at home?' and she'll say 'Oh, he's been terrible' and I'll say 'Well unfortunately he's not had a good day at school either.' It's *extremely* difficult, you know, the fine balance. I tend to give him ... average [ratings on a chart]. (Interview 13)

I think she just dreaded coming in because of what we would say about him. (Interview 16)

Surmounting the barriers

Not only did the interventions lead to a teacher perception of improved behaviour on the part of the pupil, there was also a frequent sense of resolution of some of the boundary uncertainties, usually expressed in terms of an increase in the level of 'support' from parents. Table 10.1 presents a number of examples of this in the form of comments about the level of 'support' before and after the intervention.

Table 10.1   Perceived changes in the level of support from parents before and after the intervention

Before EP involvement (Interview 18)
Darren's mum had been very critical of how he had been handled ... she's got a hair trigger.
After intervention
Mum came in every single night to check.... I think she feels the more help she gets the better.

Before EP involvement (Interview 15)
Mum had caused so many problems here. She's a very bristly lady.
After intervention
Mum and I got on quite well ... I feel she's got some respect for what I'm trying to do for him.

Before EP involvement (Interview 20)
What we lacked before was co-operation from the parents.
After intervention
Any time I meet the parents they're very enthusiastic now.

Before EP involvement (Interview 22)
We did try to get the parents involved. We got very little support from home at that time.
After intervention
The head, after her conversations with the parents, would then come to me and say, 'They're really pleased, you know.'

Before EP involvement (Interview 6)
The mother had had such negative feelings about any involvement.
After intervention
She said 'You don't know how much you've achieved with him ...' She's so positive about the improvement.

Out of the 24 cases, 16 teachers described a significant change in the level of 'back-up'; 7 of these saw it as extreme.

Mechanisms leading to the resolution of boundary tensions

The process of actually carrying out a plan within which both parents and teachers perform certain designated or negotiated actions is usually accompanied by the informal trading of information, especially in the form of the teacher gaining additional information about the pupil's behaviour at home or about particular domestic arrangements. This latter phenomenon is attested to in 16 of the cases and can occur by three routes:

The strategy encourages regular contact between teacher or parent and this information is an incidental by-product of these meetings:

His mum came in on Fridays to check to see how he'd got on.... I think he gets a better deal at home if he was good at school. (Interview 16)

[Mum] would now come and talk to me about all sorts of things ... the marriage was a bit dicey ... [she] goes out to work full-time. (Interview 15)

It's helpful for me to talk to [EP] and mum ... because you can get more of an insight ... I mean I know a bit more about his background now so I can see the reasons why he acts like he does. (Interview 12)

Meetings are arranged for which part of the agenda is the sharing of this information:

We have frequent meetings and ... there's no holds barred, we just say how we feel.... We had no idea of the depth of the problems he was shouldering for a boy of his age. (Interview 6)

More rarely, the EP acts as a go-between, relaying this information to school:

He [EP] is the liaison between home and school. He puts me in the picture officially ... he obviously explains the problems ... he's heard or discussed with mum. (Interview 9)

Participation in a joint plan and the acquisition of this additional information is then able to contribute to the resolution of boundary tensions in one of three different ways:

An increase in shared meanings:

He would go home and talk about things at school whereas before he never mentioned school.... And the next day he would come in with books and things.... Ivan's mum ... also said she thought it should go a step further. (Interview 11)

The positive things were going home but we were also getting the positive things back. (Interview 22)

A reduction in the unpredictability of the environment:

[The meetings] help you realize what the home situation is. His mum's come in and she's been very upset because she's having a lot of trouble with the older girl. (Interview 4)

So we're getting back up from them (parents) ... they seemed quite concerned and, from talking to them, they did discipline him at home, they weren't happy with what he was doing. (Interview 8)

Now I'm quite pleased with that, the contact, the fact that she can come in and tell me not just the nice things, the not so nice things. (Interview 15)

I don't think it was his home background because he's got older and younger brothers and sisters and they were fine. So, I don't think it was parenting skills really. (Interview 21)

A clarification of the boundary location:

It was important that I could report back because his mum then could be positive and praise him at home.... All the time you're getting that feedback from home, so that definitely helps to improve his behaviour during class as well. (Interview 12)

When somebody else was supervising it they probably would see that it would be quite obvious who had let the side down if they [the parents] didn't pull their weight, if the school were following their side of the programme. (Interview 20)

Resolving an apparent paradox between attribution and action

At this stage, it is possible to detect a paradox, or knot, within the attributions that are made by the teachers towards the parents.

Despite attributing the origins of the problem behaviour to factors within the parents' control in 17 cases, despite working jointly with parents and witnessing their input in 18 cases, and despite attesting to an increased level of 'support from home' in 16 cases, parent factors are cited as actually contributing to the solution in only 4 cases. In two of these the mechanism responsible is described rather generally in terms of the 'general management' of the child, and in 2 this is elaborated more specifically as an increase in 'encouragement of the child' (see Table 8.2).

At one level, there appears to be a paradox in that teachers describe increased support from parents, often a source of real relief, yet do not attribute to them any credit for the improvements that have taken place. Why is a change of management towards more positive and contingent attention seen as contributing to success in only 4 out of 16 cases when it takes place at home, but in 13 out of 21 cases when it takes place in school? What other function might be served by this notion of 'support' or 'back-up' if its initial absence is so strongly emphasized in many cases, whilst at the same time its subsequent presence is not seen as implicated in the improvements?

Attribution theory would predict that the teachers would be likely to locate the cause of the problem with an external agency and the solution with themselves, which is indeed what happens in this study. However, accepting this attribution then becomes professionally problematic. The mechanisms seen as the most direct causes of the improvement – teacher praise, appropriate types and quantities of work, incentives and a consistent approach – are none of them complex or 'psychological' and would usually be considered to be within a teacher's professional orbit.

To attribute success to these purely and simply would carry the strong implication that the solution should have been within the repertoire of the teacher originally and give a hollow ring to earlier statements about the severity of the child's difficulties and the impossibility of an internal solution. This attribution would present another threat if these teachers asked themselves whether, if the presence of these factors is responsible for success, their prior absence might not have been at least partly responsible for the initial problem? And yet these teacher factors assume high significance in the teachers' attributions of success.

The paradox can be resolved by seeing the initial 'lack of

support', which has been recast in this discussion as a form of boundary uncertainty, as being in some way causal in preventing these simple teacher actions from being implemented. In this sense, the notion of 'support' is rhetorical, a knot, and a *post hoc* rationalization for the solution not being implemented earlier. The interviews certainly contain a strong emphasis on the initial 'lack of support' but a much-reduced position for its subsequent presence.

However, the focus upon this early state also carries with it a paradox, given the nature of the intervention. If a parent is seen to play a consistent and conscientious part in a strategy, this perception is antagonistic to the prevalent typification of the parent as someone who has difficulty managing the child or is remiss in the provision of attention and consistent management.

To reconstrue the parent more positively would damage the view of an initial lack of parental support, which in turn would lead back to a challenge to the professional competence and judgement of the teacher in the early responses to the pupil. The experience of the successful strategy threatens to set in motion just such a chain of consequences.

It is at this stage that the information gleaned *during the strategy implementation* can be used to prevent this unravelling of causal attribution with its consequent professional threat. It is used in three different ways in an elaboration or refinement of the original causal attribution:

- *The closer working relationship confirms the original parent identity.* This phenomenon does not occur very frequently but may be seen in untypical examples such as:

  All his mother's comments were how wonderful he was ... she wrote in ... all the things where he'd been very good ... that was the biggest stumbling-block. (Interview 2)

- As more information about the child's behaviour at home emerges, *the teacher's typification of the child can become reinforced*, often leading to a greater empathy with the parent.

  I felt mum and dad were as desperate as we were.... I'm sure being a mum has helped because I see things as a mum's point of view as well as a teacher's point of view. (Interview 15)

  Often it can be even worse his behaviour at home. (Interview 9)

181

3 • As more information about the home circumstances emerges, it is possible to *relocate the attribution to an absent father figure*:

> We had no idea of the depth of the problems he was shouldering for a boy of his age.... Alan's father was saying dreadful things about the mother, about what she'd done and she was evil and she was going to hell and Alan would go to hell if he behaved like his mother. (Interview 6)

Each of these three processes confirms to the teacher the exceptional nature of the case. Although a positive working relationship with parents is enjoyed in many of the cases, or increased parental enthusiasm for the actions of the school is relayed from parents by the EP, the strategy gives rise to information which is used to reinforce typifications of either the mother, the pupil or an absent father.

These typifications do not challenge the original perception of a 'lack of support', but merely refine it, and this in turn is seen as the factor that was preventing the teacher from being able to carry out some of the more 'commonsense' aspects of the strategy of her or his own volition. This chain of attributions, a defensive routine in itself, depends upon the teachers not acknowledging the parents' contribution to the strategy as being directly responsible for at least part of the solution. In this way, the strategy itself and the consultative role of the EP leads to a reduction in boundary uncertainties which in turn adds to homeostasis within the school and is perceived as representing an 'improvement'.

THE PLACE OF BEHAVIOURAL APPROACHES

The discussion in the preceding two parts of this book has ranged a long way from behavioural approaches. The grounded theory study has directed the focus far more on to the process of consultation and unveiled a complex set of issues surrounding the maintenance of a school system's boundaries, the creation of temporary alternative cultures, the characteristics of successful consultants and consultations, varying attributional systems and shifts in these, and the changing constructions of parental responsibilities and contributions. In the light of these, it is worth returning to the starting point of these discussions and asking about the specific characteristics of behavioural approaches – a set of procedures which do not on the surface appear to have anything to say about issues of this type. Do behavioural techniques in themselves actually have particular properties that enable the other organizational and psychological mechanisms to come into play? Or would a consultant be able to achieve similar outcomes using another theoretical perspective or none at all? Would common sense and a sensitive, intuitive approach be enough to produce the same effect?

The next chapter attempts to address these concerns by posing the question 'Do behavioural approaches make a *distinctive and specific* contribution?'

183

PART 4

IMPLICATIONS FOR FUTURE RESEARCH AND PRACTICE

CHAPTER 11

Do behavioural consultations make a distinctive contribution?

In order to examine the distinctive and specific contributions that behavioural consultations might bring to work with pupils displaying difficult behaviour, this chapter now returns to the survey of EPs described in Chapter 3 to investigate three major questions:

- Do the approaches used by EPs in consultations with teachers actually contain recognizably distinct forms of behavioural interventions?
- Do the EPs involved see the techniques themselves as having a specific salience or are factors to do with the consultative relationship between the EPs and teachers felt to be more crucial for success?
- Do teachers really carry out the interventions recommended to them or do they first make their own modifications and alterations?

DISTINCT INTERVENTIONS?

The extent to which behavioural consultations are built upon recognizably distinct behavioural interventions

The first decade of the use of behavioural approaches by British EPs in mainstream schools drew to a close with the approaches receiving wide support within the profession. From a questionnaire study of 291 EPs (approximately one-third of practising EPs at that time), designed to examine their professional knowledge, Quicke (1978) found that 'behaviourism' featured highly among the schools of psychology that influenced EPs. In rating either a strong or weak preference for various psychological perspectives, 76 per cent of respondents mentioned the behaviourist approach, second only out of a choice of 14 perspectives to developmental psychology.

However, with this growing interest, a major schism began to appear. On the one hand, some practitioners, in the light of teachers' reservations about the approaches, put their efforts into simplifying strategies in order to make them more acceptable within classrooms. Guided not only by the potential of behavioural approaches, but also by a pragmatism born out of their appreciation of the constraints upon teachers (EPs are required to work as teachers themselves for at least two years as part of their training), these EPs became interested in exploring how 'light' a behavioural intervention could be whilst still retaining its effectiveness.

Others, however, took the view that these approaches had established their credibility only because of their strict adherence to scientific methodology and their respect for evidence rather than personal anecdote and opinion. Because the approach was still in its infancy, it was seen to be of paramount importance to retain essential features and to continue to contribute to the expanding body of experimental findings. Pragmatic compromises were seen as a dilution of practice likely to lead to the widespread discrediting of behavioural approaches and ultimately to a rejection of highly promising methods before they had been given a proper chance to establish themselves.

After reviewing a very large collection of American literature,

Harrop (1978a) concluded that there was a danger of conflict between the need to be methodologically correct and the desire to provide useful and usable techniques. Although Harrop's published work displays careful attention to issues such as the empirical demonstration of effectiveness, he argued that too much attention in that direction might lead to studies that ended up investigating the trivial. Similarly, McNamara (1982a), whose published work has been equally conscientious in this respect, came to the conclusion that practitioners might have to accept 'soft outcome measures', particularly the judgement of teachers over whether desired changes had occurred.

At around the same time, Berger (1979) launched a strong attack upon what he saw as the undermining of the actual and potential contribution of behaviour modification by a dangerous trend towards the application by practitioners in education of a 'mindless technology' – the use of procedures divorced from their theoretical techniques and applied framework. Berger claimed he was finding that teachers whom he was interviewing had often become familiar with behavioural approaches, perhaps through attending a course, but displayed only a superficial knowledge of what a behavioural approach entailed. He strongly asserted that

> behaviour modification is not, and never has been, simply a technology. It has always had associated with it some theoretical position, or at least a set of assumptions about behaviour and behaviour change. The techniques too have been applied within a particular framework of assessment or functional analysis, recording and ongoing monitoring of changes. It is when the techniques are taught or used with little or no regard to the theory and system of application that the dangers arise.

Berger was concerned that teachers should not be encouraged to use behavioural techniques without being monitored *in vivo* by a tutor who should only gradually withdraw this supervision. Although he was very opposed to attempts to teach techniques solely by means of lectures and accompanying reading, Berger's major worries were with the presentation of such approaches as token economies and 'time out'.

The extent to which the survey results reveal a 'mindless technology'

The survey of EP practice described in Chapter 3 casts some light on this issue of a 'mindless technology'. By examining what a large sample of EPs have actually been doing with teachers it is possible to see how far Berger's concerns have been borne out in practice.

Token economies

Berger was particularly worried that these techniques might be imparted to teachers with only little attempt to monitor their use and provide adequate tutorial support. The low level of material reinforcers used by the EPs in this study, around 20 per cent (see Figure 3.1), suggests that token economies, at least for work in mainstream primary settings, are not very prevalent. From this 20 per cent and the types of reinforcers listed in Table 3.3, it would seem that at least some were tangible material rewards and that the use of token economies is therefore not widespread.

Time out

Table 3.5 indicates that time-out procedures are used in 39 per cent of programmes. In terms of Berger's concerns this is a higher figure than that for token economy procedures, although the degree to which these particular techniques were introduced without an adequate rationale for their use has not been determined in this study.

Praise and ignoring

Berger conceded that there were 'nevertheless certain aspects of the behavioural approach which we could encourage teachers to use, such as identifying and responding to the positive combined with ignoring the minor disruptions'. Figure 3.1 and Table 3.5 certainly confirm that these aspects are widely used in EPs' interventions, 87 per cent of programmes use immediate teacher praise and 72 per cent ignoring of some pupil behaviour.

Supervision and monitoring

However, Berger continued by saying that even these suggestions would be difficult to implement if a competent observer was not present to give feedback on how appropriately the techniques were being used. Table 3.8 shows that 85 per cent of EPs made visits during the implementation of the strategy, although whether these visits included feedback deriving from classroom observation is not known. This table does show that 63 per cent of programmes involved the collection of data during the intervention so, presumably, changes in pupil behaviour, or the lack of them, were at least mentioned on these visits. Figure 3.2 shows the mode for the number of visits during the implementation to be 3, with few interventions incorporating more than this. In most of these interventions the first of these visits is arranged for four weeks after commencement, as shown in Figure 3.3.

It seems reasonable to assume that this frequency is dictated more by EPs' workload pressures than considerations of ideal timings and, indeed, Table 3.15 confirms that EPs do quote constraints on their time as being the major barrier to more successful interventions. Even if these timings were felt to be ideal, it could be argued that this length of time before a first monitoring period might allow an intervention to drift from its original course or, at least, prevent initial 'teething' problems from being addressed earlier.

Although 48 per cent of interventions are reviewed within less than four weeks, it might seem that Berger's concerns about adequate supervision and monitoring are at least partly justified. However, Table 3.13 shows that whether or not monitoring visits occurred, their total number and the extent of the period before a first review *were not related to the success or otherwise of the intervention.*

In summary, the study suggests that although some of Berger's concerns may be justified, in terms of the use of time out and perhaps the level of supervision, others, in particular the implementation of token economies, are not. However, Berger is concerned with remaining faithful to the behavioural method, believing, perhaps reasonably, that dilutions are likely to lead to the discrediting of approaches capable of assisting teachers and pupils. If, in fact, organizational and attributional processes are as, or more, important for behavioural consultants, then strict adherence may not be considered so important. In order to shed some light on this aspect, this chapter now examines another area of the data from the survey of EPs.

TECHNIQUES OR RELATIONSHIPS?

The extent to which the EPs involved see the behavioural techniques themselves rather than the consultative relationship as being more crucial for success

In addition to examining the way in which EPs actually construct programmes with teachers, the possibly distinctive contributions of behavioural *consultations* may be illuminated by also looking at what the EPs see as specifically 'psychological' about the interventions.

After the main body of the questionnaire described in chapter 3, EPs were therefore asked a far more open-ended question in an attempt to ascertain their views on this matter. Specifically, they were asked, '*For the types of school and children's problems examined in this questionnaire, which aspect(s) of devising and implementing a behavioural approach do you feel most require the skills and/or knowledge of a psychologist?*'

The results showed EPs to be almost evenly divided over the issue of the psychological skills necessary to work with primary school teachers on behavioural approaches. One-half see their expertise purely, or at least primarily, in terms of the 'behavioural methodology' (e.g. stating the problem in behavioural terms, task analysis, reinforcement schedules, etc.), while the remainder see consultative skills as of equal, or more, importance (see Table 11.1). Indeed, about one-fifth did not even mention knowledge of programme construction as among the most significant skills they brought to these interventions. It is, of course, quite probable that more respondents would have listed more items if they had been encouraged to do so. However, when asked to give their view of the *most important* skills and knowledge that psychologists bring to this work, these were considered the most salient features.

Table 11.1 **The aspects of devising and implementing a behavioural approach that most require the skills and/or knowledge of a psychologist** *(N=62)*

	Percentage of respondents
'Behavioural methodology' only	47
'Behavioural methodology' plus consultative aspects	36
Consultative aspects only	18

The most frequently mentioned 'technological' aspects were the stating of the problem in behavioural terms, selection of appropriate reinforcers, and the creation of a monitoring or recording system. The other aspects of applying programmes requiring the skills or knowledge of a psychologist – the consultative aspects – were identified by respondents as 'working with the emotional climate', that is, countering mistrust, absorbing negative emotions and 'selling' the intervention. In addition, *the ability to explain* specialist knowledge, especially in terms of identifying causative and maintaining factors for behaviour, a knowledge of what is feasible in classrooms, and being aware of issues associated with role, such as avoiding the assumption of total 'ownership' of a problem, were also quoted.

These results show that, within the widely used behavioural approach, some practitioners consider the 'psychological' component of their interventions to lie in the actual construction of the behavioural interventions that they make available for teachers to use with certain pupils, whereas others see psychology's main emphasis to lie in the actual interactions they have with the teachers.

There would thus appear to be a group of 'hard-nosed behaviourists' within the profession – about 50 per cent of all EPs who use these approaches see the theoretical rationale as deriving from behavioural psychology and see no problem with this as an explanatory framework. Conversely, the other 50 per cent who use the approaches see the real contribution of psychology to lie in the assistance the discipline gives to the EP to participate in a consultative relationship.

But do these two groups experience different rates of success? Does a firm adherence to the technology of behavioural interventions produce better outcomes, as the literature reviewed in Chapter 2 suggests? Or does an explicit attention to the practical and attributional concerns of teachers yield better returns? Table 11.2 analyses the different outcome results for these two groups of practitioners.

Table 11.2   The rates of success experienced by practitioners informed by different theoretical perspectives *(N=56)*

	Percentage of programmes	
	Considerable improvement	Moderate or no improvement
Strict adherents	38	62
Others	37	63

The proportion of respondents who achieve 'considerable success' in each group is amazingly similar, just over one-third, demonstrating that the EPs' theoretical rationale does not lead to differential outcomes.

The discussion in this chapter so far rests upon the reports furnished by the EPs in their questionnaire replies. What if the teachers for whom these interventions were devised did not actually implement them in the ways suggested? This could mean the spread of an even more accentuated form of 'mindless technology' or the teachers' modifications could hold the key to the distinctive elements of behavioural consultations.

INTENTIONS AND OUTCOMES

The extent to which teachers really carry out the recommended interventions and the extent to which they first make their own modifications and alterations

Before tackling this question directly it is worth remembering that there is a substantial literature, some of which has been reviewed in Chapter 2, to demonstrate that behavioural approaches can have a positive effect upon the behaviour of pupils in schools. However, as Chapter 4 has also shown, EPs working as consultants have frequently encountered difficulties in encouraging teachers to take up their recommendations and have often found that even successful interventions do not lead to teachers, those actually involved as well as their colleagues, using such approaches again of their own volition when similar problems arise. Parts 2 and 3 of this book have pursued the organizational and attributional processes that are implicated in this lack of take-up and generalization among teachers.

A major question remains. Do behavioural approaches have particular characteristics that allow consultants and teachers to work productively together? Table 8.6 showed that 87 per cent of the teachers in this study thought that pupils' behaviour improved because of actions within their control, and Table 8.4 identified the most prominent of these to be their giving of positive attention to the pupil, setting work of an appropriate interest level, splitting tasks into sequences of steps and using rewards or incentives. To explore which aspects of the advice they were given these teachers used, it is necessary to return to the teacher interviews, particularly the answers to the question, 'Can you tell me about the things the EP suggested?' – both the immediate answers and those following prompts. Table 11.3 summarizes this data.

One of the most immediate implications arising from this list is the relatively low application by teachers of the three main elements of a behavioural approach as originally incorporated in the study by Madsen *et al.* (1968) and employed extensively since – the use of praise, ignoring and attention to rules. Even with prompts in respect of these items, a chi-squared test reveals that for all three elements teacher usage fell significantly below the level of EPs' recommendations, as determined from the questionnaire in Chapter 3. Table 11.4 compares the percentage of programmes recommended by surveyed EPs containing these three elements with the percentage of interviewed teachers who said that these were recommended by the EP. The statistical comparisons are between the EPs' recommendations and the teachers' memory of including the elements after being prompted about the items.

Table 11.3   Teachers' recollections of the elements of strategies recommended by the EPs

	Number of cases	
	Immediate answers	With prompts
Charts with steps/sections of the day, etc.	9	0
Home/school diaries/records	7	4
Ignoring certain behaviour	5	6
Praise/positive attention	6	4
Elaboration/decisions about rules	5	1
Moving child's seating position	3	1
Setting targets/steps to target	3	0
Joint teacher/pupil recording	3	0
Time out (including sat elsewhere briefly)	2	2
Home/school meetings	2	0
Using explicit rewards	2	0
Involving other children	1	0
Record-keeping	1	1
Reading programme	1	0
Checklist for belongings	1	0
Response cost	1	0
Changing original targets	0	2
Consistent approach across staff	1	0
Eye-to-eye contact	1	0
Contract	1	0
List problems and prioritize	1	0
Environmental analysis	1	0
Use of sanctions	1	0
Involving other staff	1	0
Restraint	1	0
Class rewards	0	1

Table 11.4   The percentage rates of inclusion of the elements – teacher praise, ignoring and attention to rules – in the programmes recommended by EPs and those actually implemented by teachers

	EPs ($N=68$)	Teacher (immediate)	Teacher (incl. prompted) ($N=24$)	Significance
Praise	87	25	42	0.001
Ignoring	72	21	46	0.05
Attention to rules	51	21	25	0.05

This raises at least two major implications for the present study. Firstly, it demands that the data presented in Part 1 are very much treated as the constructions and intentions of EPs rather than a 'true' reflection of the actions carried out by the teachers. Table 11.4 reaffirms how necessary it is to continue to emphasize this.

The second major implication is that the success of the interventions investigated in these teacher interviews is unlikely to be due, in the main, to the application of behavioural psychology, as only minimal applications can be seen to have taken place, thus throwing the onus of explanation back on to such processes as boundary maintenance and the management of attribution shift as described above.

But does the EP really attribute the success of interventions specifically to the behavioural aspects of the intervention rather than interpersonal factors within the consultative relationship? Would any framework that granted the EP enough confidence to begin have served an equal purpose, with the mechanisms discussed above finding their way almost inevitably into the intervention once begun?

This study suggests that the answer to these two questions is probably 'No'. Behavioural approaches in themselves appear to have qualities that enable them to achieve outcomes that might be denied to less theoretically inclined, 'commonsense' approaches, or to those deriving from other theoretical perspectives.

The behavioural approach places an emphasis upon tasks. So too do a number of writers from the ecosystemic paradigm, even if the main theoretical focus of their attentions is upon the interactions between the members of two systems. Dallos (1991) has argued that in therapy with family groups 'behaving and construing must proceed together' and Taylor (1982) has pointed out that tasks that involve both the school and the family can help to change the dysfunctional interaction between the two systems. Even in the 25 per cent of cases where parents and teachers do not work directly together, the EP is still involved in the crucial task of relaying information between the two systems and effecting the interaction, as it were, by proxy.

Given the nature of the attributions that surround the difficult behaviour of pupils, and the intensity of the emotions that often accompany these, an approach that is able to deflect from, or sidestep, these in the initial stages is likely to have a chance at least to begin. Approaches by the EP that appear to be 'siding' with either parents or teachers are likely further to enflame feelings of blame and hostility. Additional problems for approaches employing more direct attention to the probably conflicting accounts from home and school, and attempting to work with the constructions of parents and teachers, are highlighted in Aponte's (1976) warning that teachers do not like to be treated like clients, especially when brought together with parents. A behavioural approach deflects attention from these aspects on to the formulation of target behaviours and the like, followed either by baseline recording or the direct implementation of a strategy.

Furthermore, the contributions required by strategies from both parents and teachers are likely to be relatively small and reasonably equitably balanced, thus enabling each party to begin to demonstrate to the other their concern to achieve positive outcomes for the pupil whilst not feeling they are being unreasonably 'saddled' with duties that are the responsibility of the other. When this demonstration occurs, even in those cases where the EP is acting as a go-between, then the parents and teachers are able to validate their own positions in the eyes of the other. As this mutual validation grows with the progress of the strategy, the intensity of accusatory feelings diminishes and the EP is able to employ a range of interpersonal skills to help establish a new system characterized by a greater degree of mutual understanding and tolerance and within which various shifts in attribution can take place.

The penultimate chapter will now present formally the grounded theory that has been developed, in an attempt to pull together and summarize the major strands to have emerged from the studies described in this book. The final chapter will bring the discussion back to current professional challenges and seek to learn the practical lessons presented by this study.

CHAPTER 12

Implications for theoretical development

This chapter summarizes the grounded theory that has been developed within the preceding chapters.

THE FORMAL STATEMENT OF THE GROUNDED THEORY

Schools as organizations maintain their function and purpose partly through activities designed to define and validate their boundary with their environment (Glatter, 1989). Clear boundary definition promotes internal stability, homeostasis (Rice, 1976), and allows for the generation of norms and rules to address such issues as the procedures for interacting with other system members, dealing with internally disruptive events, carrying out joint tasks, and communicating across the boundary.

Within schools, the task of teaching leads to differences from many other work roles in terms of the extent and nature of collegiate behaviour (Little, 1990). Although teacher colleagues may well provide a range of affiliative functions, they do not serve as stimuli and agents for each other's professional development (Little, 1990). Instead, teachers draw on reference groups who provide internal frames of reference through which to structure their perceptual field in respect of professional issues (Nias, 1985). These reference groups, whose members will be construed as 'like-minded', may be very small, perhaps consisting of only one other colleague who may be as likely to be external as internal to the school.

A number of features of schools and the work role of teachers contribute to this relative professional isolation: the ecology of most schools; the major reward for teachers being the development and response of pupils (Lortie, 1975), which is most easily earned away from colleagues; the lack of a technical language with which teachers may discuss their work (Lortie, 1975); the lack of a commonly agreed standard by which teachers may measure their own worth and hence increase their confidence; and the high value placed upon being able to keep a class under control, leading to a reluctance to be observed and the desire for a more physically bounded space (Little, 1990; Lieberman and Miller, 1990).

The task of teaching can require rapid sequences of decision-making and, although teachers may employ an accounting system that is professional and theoretical in its vocabulary, the immediacy, frequency and changing nature of classroom demands can lead to their actions being more governed by '*ad hoc*ing' and the following of 'tried and tested' routines (Sharp and Green, 1975).

In settings where a number of teachers meet particular pupils, conversations between teacher colleagues, in the absence of a shared technical language, can serve as vehicles for the trading of summary typifications (Hammersley, 1984). Such typifications, which are predominantly concerned with pupil behaviour seen as difficult, can be used by teachers to guide their behaviour in the immediacy of the classroom. Rather than promoting a consideration of contextual factors, these typifications are presented as stable psychological characteristics of pupils (Hammersley, 1984). Despite a shared construction of a pupil among staff, however, teachers often report a high degree of isolation in terms of feeling responsible for that pupil's management.

When a pupil's behaviour is perceived as presenting a management challenge of a severe nature, various attributional processes are employed to account for this. The degree of differentiation within a set of attributions represents the extent of its conceptual elaboration and hence its importance (Eiser, 1978). In this respect, teachers possess a highly differentiated set of explanatory mechanisms relating to children, about twice as many as associated with themselves, with the number attributed to parents lying at an intermediary level.

Among the more frequent explanatory mechanisms attributed to pupils for difficult behaviour are physical or medical factors, a need for praise, a lack of acceptance of social norms and temperament or personality. The most common attributions to parents are general child-management strategies, a punitive or violent home, an absent father, and a lack of attention. Predominant causes attributed by teachers to themselves consist of setting insufficiently interesting work and having unrealistic expectations of the pupil.

However, the extent to which those who act are perceived as not responsible for their actions and are thus deserving of sympathy and help is governed by the degree of controllability judged to exist in their actions (Weiner, 1980). In the case of 'difficult pupil behaviour', parents are judged as being about twice as responsible as pupils for this behaviour, with teachers this time lying at an intermediary level.

Attributing the responsibility for a pupil's difficult behaviour to parents, however, introduces boundary uncertainties within the organization, because the responsibility for pupil behaviour within the system is being located outside. Because teachers and parents may construe their respective responsibilities and attribute causation differently, the exact location of the boundary, its definition, becomes less certain, thus risking a decrease in the organization's homeostasis. Teachers' uncertainties over the predictability of the environment itself, in such terms as perceived alien parental lifestyle or maturity, further exacerbate the boundary tension and act as a barrier to its resolution.

The involvement of an EP can lead to outcomes perceived by the teacher as highly positive. This is achieved by means of the creation of a new system whose membership includes at least the teacher, the EP and one parent, and sometimes other school staff and family members. Within the boundary of this system, new norms and rules are created and, because of the incorporation of the external consultant, this may be seen as a 'therapeutic suprasystem' (De Shazer, 1982).

This suprasystem has two distinctive features. Firstly, it is seen as temporary and existing by virtue of the presence of the EP. As a result, notions of the EP's 'involvement' become the legitimization for the new norms and procedures. Secondly, it overlaps the other two systems of school and family and allows its members to belong to both the new and their original systems and adhere to both sets of norms and values simultaneously, even when these are contradictory. These 'knots' in teachers' thinking are especially likely to occur in relation to colleagues (Wagner, 1987). Teachers frequently report on levels of emotional support and a developing intersubjectivity between members of the new system that approximate to their experience within reference groups.

Various routes may be taken in the creation of the new temporary overlapping system. The most common starting point is for the EP to bring together a parent or parents with the teacher and possibly other members of staff. Working intensively with either the teacher or a parent separately is also a frequent early strategy for the EP. Systems may include members who never all meet together, in which case information and judgements are transferred between home and school by the EP. In the majority of interventions the final state is for parents and teachers to be working together in some way without the presence of the EP, although the 'involvement' of the EP may still be invoked as the factor making it possible for teachers to construe or behave 'untypically' towards parents.

Particular forms of knowledge, skills, personal qualities and aspects of role are seen by teachers to be the distinctive features of EPs' involvement. In particular, knowledge derived from practice is valued above that with an established research base and there is a reluctance on the part of teachers to incorporate levels of abstraction into their discussions. EPs, on the contrary, commonly regard the research base within applied behavioural analysis as providing at least a part of the rationale for their contribution. Listening and problem-solving skills on the part of EPs are regarded as important by the teachers. Taking an encouraging and approving stance and avoiding being directive are all singled out as being significant qualities in facilitating the social *climate*

interaction and non-attributive nature of meetings involving both teachers and parents.

The applied behavioural analysis paradigm provides the rationale for the strategies developed within these suprasystems, although a sizeable minority see an amalgam of interactional and interpretive skills as their true professional contribution as psychologists. Widely-researched components such as teacher praise, ignoring and clear statements of rules (e.g. Madsen *et al.*, 1968) are frequently included in the strategies they recommend but are consciously implemented by the teachers to a significantly lesser degree.

Although implemented less often than recommended, discussion of the practicalities surrounding these tasks nevertheless gives a rationale for bringing together parties who are highly likely to be in a position of mutual blaming and hostility. Relatively small and equitably balanced requirements from both parents and teachers create a climate in which each can see that the other is making a contribution, thus validating the purpose for meeting and reducing the need for defensive negative attributions towards the other party.

Teachers who achieve success in this manner – and the 'behavioural' component of their strategies is often fairly minimal and imprecise – can experience a degree of change characterized by movement from 'the most difficult pupil encountered in twelve years' to 'a remarkable success story'. Their new construction of the pupil, however, threatens to disrupt the typification that has often been co-created between the various members of staff familiar with the pupil, especially by virtue of having been a class teacher in a previous year. Although many schools have devised or are in the process of devising whole-school behaviour policies – the espoused theory (Argyris and Schon, 1978) – the culture of many schools, the system of informal rules that spell out how people are to behave most of the time (Deal and Kennedy, 1982), or the theory in use in respect of managing pupil behaviour, often remain antagonistic to notions of teachers being able to effect change.

For a teacher, widely acknowledged successful outcomes with a pupil are likely to strain affiliative relationships with colleagues. Consequently, the boundary of the suprasystem serves not only to define the new set of norms and values that will apply to working with a particular pupil, it also insulates the rest of the school from these undertakings. Clear evidence of changed pupil behaviour would challenge typifications of deviant identity that consolidate the culture in respect of difficult behaviour, thus decreasing the homeostasis of the organization. By keeping EP strategies separate from the rest of the school's procedures, and in existence only as long as the temporary EP 'involvement' applies, the school's usual procedures, the theory in action, can be maintained. Implications for possible changes in the way parents are construed do not impinge, thus validating the school's existing boundary and preserving homeostasis.

By working directly with parents or receiving reports on their contributions and (positive) reactions via the EPs, teachers experience a lessening of boundary tensions. This comes about in three ways. Firstly, by carrying out a joint strategy the opportunity exists for an increase in shared meanings, one of the most significant being that the purpose of meeting is to carry out and monitor certain tasks rather than engage in conversations that carry heavy implication of blame. Secondly, the location of the boundary is clarified and the teacher achieves a greater confidence in knowing which areas are the responsibility of whom. And thirdly, environmental uncertainties are reduced for the teacher as aspects of the parents' motivation and lifestyle become more clearly understood.

Despite working together and witnessing the contribution made to strategies by parents, teachers rarely attribute to the parents any credit for the perceived improvement. Neither do they see factors within the pupils' control as frequently responsible either. Instead, they are around five times more likely to see themselves, rather than the parents, as having effected the change. The most common mechanism invoked for this is their positive attention to the child.

This causal attribution carries with it a threat. If these teacher-directed activities are mainly responsible for the success, the implication is that their earlier absence may have played some part in the genesis of the problem or that, at the least, they should have been enacted earlier. Whilst this contradiction may usually be contained within a knot in a teacher's thinking (Wagner, 1987), circumstances may confront the teacher with the need to reconcile this implied threat to professionalism.

An initial 'lack of parental support' is frequently invoked as the barrier to implementing a solution earlier. Subsequent 'parental support' and the parent's direct contribution to the strategy, are not credited in themselves with having any effect. Instead, the experience of working with a parent, whilst bringing a sense of lessened anxiety through the reduction of boundary tensions, is also used to reinforce the notion of an earlier 'lack of support' as being responsible for the absence of earlier positive action.

This reinforcement takes place in one of three ways. The first and least common mechanism is the confirmation of the original parent identity. More commonly, as more information emerges during the course of working together it becomes possible to relocate the attribution to an absent father. Alternatively, the mother is absolved from a direct responsibility as more information about home is included in conversations and the teacher increasingly attributes the origins of the difficulties to factors concerning the child which are not within the child's control.

The adoption of medical models in respect of pupils and enlightenment models (Fiske and Taylor, 1984) associated with absent fathers allows teachers to protect their professional self-esteem from implied accusations of a lack of early positive action and to attribute to themselves much of the credit for improvements in the pupils' behaviour. At the same time, the lessening of boundary tensions, achievable by virtue of having first escaped temporarily from school cultures surrounding deviant pupil behaviour, leads to a greater sense of professional self-confidence and emotional well-being.

CHAPTER 13

Implications for practice in schools

Although the chapters in this book draw upon a theoretical literature, many of the lessons for practice in schools should
nevertheless be relatively apparent. Rather than reiterating every
point, this concluding chapter will therefore discuss a selection
of the key implications for teachers, headteachers and outside
consultants.

The major practical lesson to emerge from this study is that
primary school teachers are able to bring about positive changes
in the behaviour of some of their most difficult pupils. This
point needs to be made emphatically at the outset. Headlines
and rhetoric, both political and professional, gravitate almost
inevitably towards the sensational and the pessimistic. Morale
in schools is further undermined by the relentless bombardment
of criticism and bad news. Of course, casual and unsubstanti-
ated claims that teachers can easily, and therefore should
without any help, eliminate difficult pupil behaviour can be
equally undermining. This study has shown that, although
teachers can be highly effective, there are a number of subtle and
potentially delicate processes that may need to be addressed
before these positive outcomes can be achieved.

The first part of the book has shown that success in using
behavioural approaches is not confined to the 'demonstration

studies' in the research and professional literature. In less than ideal circumstances, within the resource politics of professional referral settings, with teachers who feel isolated or severely undermined, it is possible to bring about change with some of the most difficult pupils in primary schools. Among the most frequently occurring elements in these interventions (see Table 3.12) are classroom observation by EPs, defining pupil behaviour in observable terms, selecting target behaviours to increase, and the use of immediate teacher praise as a reinforcer. However, Table 3.13 pinpoints classroom rules and their careful formulation and explanation to pupils as a particularly essential feature of successful programmes.

The studies described in Part 1 provide a rich selection of targets and strategies which may be incorporated into stages of the Code of Practice. However, Berger's (1979) warnings about mindless technologies are pertinent in this respect. If teachers in schools select only one or two elements from the repertoire of behavioural strategies – and the Code in many ways encourages early, relatively 'simple' interventions – and if these are not effective, then there is an increased likelihood that subsequent, potentially effective strategies recommended by special needs co-ordinators (SENCOs), behaviour support teachers or EPs may receive less enthusiastic welcomes within classrooms. In many ways, Berger's misgivings are more appropriate to the current context than they were to the activities of EPs and teachers in the late 1970s.

Of course, the process of consultation is as much, or more, concerned with factors to do with the changing relationship between the teacher, EP, parent and child as it is to do with the characteristics of any particular strategy. Figure 9.1 attempts to summarize this finding in diagrammatic form. And although it has been possible to isolate a few core elements of strategies that appear to be essential for success, Chapter 11 has demonstrated that teachers often alter recommended strategies anyway or, at least, do not necessarily rate these elements as being of primary significance.

The success of such approaches, even when seemingly reduced to their bare essentials, must, however, be set within the massive paradox that surrounds behavioural consultations. Whereas earlier proponents had identified the problems of generalization of behavioural practice within schools, the actual role of staff culture has been much more clearly delineated by the research reported here. Behavioural approaches, especially modern adaptations that have tackled issues such as pupil control versus autonomy, the early over-emphasis on on-task behaviour, and the over-reliance on consequences, strongly encourage a problem-solving approach (see Chapter 2). This study has shown clearly that problem-solving in respect of difficult pupil behaviour is not a prevalent feature of the staff cultures in at least some schools.

The strong implication arising from this study for those who work in and with schools is that a way must be found to influence and manage staff culture in respect of difficult pupil behaviour. As organizations, schools are not alone in this difficult enterprise. Following his early work with a range of organizations, both in the public and private sector, Checkland (1994) revised his soft systems methodology to address issues of culture more explicitly. Earlier formulations, which dealt far more with stated, policy-directed procedures, were seen to founder on the rock of cultural resistance, thus necessitating approaches that addressed both policy and culture simultaneously. Similarly, but specifically related to schools, Dalin's (1993) Institutional Development Programme has been used in over a thousand schools in many parts of the world. This is an approach to school improvement involving an external consultant whose long-range goal is to move a school towards becoming a learning culture. The clearly specified and detailed sequence of procedures, because it is concerned with changing culture, focuses upon the subjective reality of the school as experienced by its staff members as much as upon the objective reality in terms of its formal organization and written procedures.

The projects described in Chapter 7 show that British EPs have historically had an interest in working with schools as organizations; the theoretical roots of this practice are in systems theories and process consultation. However, it has been very difficult for this professional group to resolve the problem of being typecast as predominantly or exclusively concerned with casework focused upon individual pupils and their teachers and parents. The legal requirement for EPs to contribute to the Code of Practice is the latest major reinforcement of this perspective. There has never been a similar legal requirement for organizational work.

Superficially, it can be argued that there should not be an exclusivity, one way or the other. But the stereotype of the EP as a quasi-medical professional has proved impossible to shift in the minds of many in education, not only those working in schools but also those involved in policy formulation and the drafting of legislation. The present study has shown that these individual approaches can bring success, but that the input of consultative work required to bring about such results is intensive. The lack of generalization, brought about by homeostatic and boundary aspects of schools and the attributional processes of teachers, also means that successful individual interventions are unlikely to build a body of knowledge and skill within schools so that more preventive and less intensive involvements may achieve similar results in the future.

In view of this, there is a need for EPs involved in individual interventions of this type to consider setting up clearer expectations at the outset. Teachers do not have a great deal of time in which to reflect upon practice, and cultural factors do not encourage this in respect of difficult behaviour. Because the involvement of an EP as an external consultant represents a considerable resource investment, there is an economic, as well as a professional, need to maximize the impact of interventions.

This could be achieved by EPs making explicit before undertaking any strategy-planning with a school that mechanisms must exist so that lessons learned during an individual intervention can be generalized within the school. In particular, EPs will need to make sure that opportunities will exist for the teachers they work with to have time to consider and correctly attribute the causal factors at work during interventions. Similarly, time will need to be made available so that teachers can also be supported while they clarify the generalizable skills and knowledge that they have learned and the ways they might use them with other pupils in the future. Beyond the individual classroom, headteachers and SENCOs might also be asked to commit themselves beforehand to learning about the ways in which generalizable skills and knowledge can be shared across the whole school staff and subsequently employed by other teachers. In order for some of these aims to be achieved, it is probable that the lessons from the present research about organizational and attributional processes will also need to be made explicit and familiar to schools.

The key challenge is to find a way in which the cultures created within the temporary overlapping boundaries that result from the successful involvement of EPs can be generated more easily from within schools. The research reported in this book has shown that, in order to work effectively in these circumstances, teachers may need to experience some or all of the following:

- meetings which are managed in such a way that high degrees of anxiety and hostility are resolved;
- the modelling of certain ways of listening and asking questions;
- new ways of construing parents and children;
- an opportunity to reconsider attributions for the origins of difficult behaviour and the mechanisms underlying possible changes;
- temporary removal from the obligation to assert school policy;
- a sense of shared responsibility with other professionals;
- exposure to strategies that incorporate equitable commitments to small steps on the part of both parents and teachers;
- a knowledge of the principles underlying behavioural approaches and the ways in which practice has evolved in response to the contributions made by school-based personnel.

Somehow those responsible for organizing the approach a school takes towards the difficult behaviour of some of its pupils need to address these issues. This is a serious challenge for headteachers and SENCOs, not because they do not possess, or are unable to acquire, the necessary skills and knowledge, but because a number of these factors depend upon role relationships. Some are far harder for a member of a school's staff – any member – to enact. The need for a strong collaboration between school personnel and external support agencies, with a clear differentiation of their roles, would thus seem to be self-evident.

The policies developed by schools in respect of pupil behaviour are crucial but they will be of little consequence if not backed up by highly supportive cultures. Headteachers need to facilitate peer support and networking between teachers, not only within individual schools but also clusters of schools where it should be possible to step outside the cultures of specific organizations. These meetings should serve the function of allowing teachers to share their successes, ventilate emotions and decrease their sense of isolation, thus increasing the opportunity for teachers to develop a professional reference group. Such groups may need facilitating, at least in their early stages, by external consultants operating in the ways developed by Osborne (1983), Hanko (1990), Stringer *et al.* (1992) and others (see Chapter 7).

The competing explanatory frameworks outlined in Chapter 1, school effectiveness and classroom management approaches versus the problem-child paradigm, still struggle to find some form of compatibility and co-existence. Advocates from one camp can often find little by way of dialogue with the other. Ironically, perhaps, for all the initial and continuing misgivings that surround behavioural approaches, these techniques have advanced the conciliation. From their origins within the professional interests of groups firmly allied with making provision for the most difficult pupils, these approaches have been drawn bit by bit into the realms of school and classroom organization.

A solid research and practice base for work with and in schools will be all the more necessary if the war of attribution over pupil behaviour continues to escalate. The crude and simplistic blaming of teachers, pupils or parents, alternating as the merry-go-round of political fashion grinds on, must be countered, if only because professional optimism and clear-headedness is so unlikely to rise from a pit of demoralization. Equally, over-zealous pursuit of medical model attributions, as evidenced by the rise to prominence of attention-deficit disorder and other 'syndrome approaches', may also leave professionals, parents and pupils themselves feeling that their own actions may be of little or no benefit.

In conclusion, it seems likely that EPs will continue to argue for an approach which addresses organizational issues and, now especially, organizational culture, as well as individual interventions. While crusades against undesirable pupil behaviour sit easily within the political lexicon, notions concerning the influence of culture and attribution require a little more thought and reflection. Examples of successful consultations exist and their underlying mechanisms have been clarified. With the potential for all parties to benefit, with successful outcomes for teachers, pupils, parents and EPs realizable, the time must surely have arrived for a reappraisal of approaches to difficult behaviour in schools, in order to displace empty rhetoric and uninformed opinion and draw instead on the growing body of research into successful practice.

References

Aponte, H. J. (1976) The family–school interview: an eco-structural approach. *Family Process*, **15**, 303–11.

Argyris, C. and Schon, D. (1978) *Organizational Learning*. Reading, MA: Addison-Wesley.

Atkeson, B. M. and Forehand, R. (1979) Home-based reinforcement programs designed to modify classroom behaviour: a review and methodological evaluation. *Psychological Bulletin*, **86**(6), 1298–1308.

Aubrey, C. (1987) Training for the role of school consultant as a means of dealing effectively with behaviour problems in schools. *Educational and Child Psychology*, **4**(2), 14–29.

Axelrod, S., Moyer, L. and Berry, B. (1990) Why teachers do not use behaviour modification procedures. *Journal of Educational and Psychological Consultation*, **1**(4), 309–20.

Ball, S. J. (1987) *The Micro-politics of the School*. London: Methuen.

Barth, R. (1979) Home-based reinforcement of school behaviour: A review and analysis. *Review of Educational Research*, **49**(3), 436–58.

Bergan, J. R. and Neumann, A. J. (1980) The identification of resources and constraints influencing plan design in consultation. *Journal of School Psychology*, **18**, 317–23.

Bergan, J. R. and Tombari, M. L. (1976) Consultant skill and efficiency and the implementation and outcomes of consultation. *Journal of School Psychology*, **14**, 3–14.

Bergan, J. R., Byrnes, I. M. and Kratochwill, T. R. (1979). Effects of behavioural and medical models of consultation on teacher expectancies and instruction of a hypothetical child. *Journal of School Psychology*, **17**, 307–16.

Berger, M. (1979) Behaviour modification in education and professional practice: the dangers of a mindless technology. *Bulletin of the British Psychological Society*, **32**, 418–19.

Berger, M., Yule, W. and Wigley, V. (1987) The teacher–child interaction project: implementing behavioural programmes with troublesome individual children in the primary school. In K. Wheldall (ed.), *The Behaviourist in the Classroom*. London: Allen and Unwin.

Berger, P. and Luckman, T. (1966) *The Social Construction of Reality*. London: Penguin.

Bradley, G. and McNamara, E. (1981) The structured treatment of problem behaviour: prevention is better than cure. *Behavioural Approaches with Children*, **5**(4), 4–12.

Bridges, D. (1987) 'It's the ones who never turn up that you really want to see'. The 'problem' of the non-attending parent. In J. Bastiani (ed.), *Parents and Teachers 1*. Slough: NFER.

Bull, S. L. and Solity, J. E. (1989) *Classroom Management: Principles to Practice*. London: Routledge.

Burden, R. L. (1974) Teaching teachers about reading problems: the need for involvement at every level. *Remedial Education*, **9**(3), 132–4.

Burden, R. L. (1976) Training educational psychologists to work in schools: the Exeter approach. *Remedial Education*, **11**(2), 61–8.

Burden, R. L. (1978) Schools' systems analysis: a project-centred approach. In B. Gillham (ed.), *Reconstructing Educational Psychology*. London: Croom Helm.

Burden, R. L. (1981) The educational psychologist as instigator and agent of change in schools: some guidelines for successful practice. In I. McPherson and A. Sutton (eds), *Reconstructing Psychological Practice*. London: Croom Helm.

Burland, P. M. and Burland, J. R. (1979) ... and teacher came too! *Behavioural Psychotherapy*, **7**(1), 7–11.

Burland, R. (1979) Social skills as the basis for coping strategies in school. *Proceedings of the 1979 DECP Annual Course*. British Psychological Society.

Caffyn, R. E. (1987) Rewards and punishments in schools. A study of their effectiveness as perceived by secondary school pupils and their teachers. *School Psychology International*, **8**, 85–94.

Caffyn, R. E. (1989) Attitudes of British secondary school teachers and pupils to rewards and punishments. *Educational Research*, **31**(3), 210–20.

Cameron, R. J. and Stratford, R. J. (1978) Target practice: aiming at professional accountability. *Occasional Papers of the Division of Educational and Child Psychology*, **3**(2), 47–59.

Campion, J. (1984) Psychological services for children: using family therapy in the setting of a school psychological service. *Journal of Family Therapy*, **6**, 47–62.

Cannell, C. F. and Kahn, R. L. (1968) Interviewing. In G. Lindzey and E. Aronson (eds), *The Handbook of Social Psychology* (2nd edition). Reading, MA: Addison-Wesley.

Canter, L. and Canter, M. (1992) *Lee Canter's Assertive Discipline: Positive Behaviour Management for Today's Classroom*. Santa Monica, CA: Canter and Associates.

Caplan, G. (1970) *An Approach to Community Mental Health*. London: Tavistock (cited in J. C. Conoley and C. W. Conoley, 1990).

Checkland, P. (1994) Systems theory and management thinking. *American Behavioral Scientist*, **38**(1), 75–91.

Cheeseman, P. L. and Watts, P. E. (1985) *Positive Behaviour Management: A Manual for Teachers*. London: Croom Helm.

Chisholm, B., Kearney, D., Knight, G., Little, H., Morris, S. and Tweddle, D. (1986) *Preventative Approaches to Disruption*. Basingstoke: Macmillan Education.

Conoley, J. C. and Conoley, C. W. (1990) Staff consultative work in schools. In N. Jones and N. Frederickson (eds), *Refocusing Educational Psychology*. Basingstoke: Falmer.

Cooper, P. and Upton, G. (1990) An ecosystemic approach to emotional and behavioural difficulties in school. *Educational Psychology*, **10**(4), 301–21.

Cooper, P. and Upton, G. (1991) Controlling the urge to control: An ecosystemic approach to problem behaviour in schools. *Support for Learning*, **6**(1), 22–6.

Coulby, D. and Harper, T. (1985) *Preventing Classroom Disruption. Policy, Practice and Evaluation in Urban Schools*. London: Croom Helm.

Cox, K. (1982) INSET with a complete school staff to help reactions to change. *Occasional Papers of the Division of Educational and Child Psychology*, **6**(1), 50–5.

Croll, P. and Moses, D. (1985) *One in Five. The Assessment and Incidence of Special Educational Needs*. London: Routledge and Kegan Paul.

Dalin, P. (1993) *Changing the School Culture*. London: Cassell.

Dallos, R. (1991) *Family Belief Systems, Therapy and Change*. Milton Keynes: Open University Press.

Daniels, T. D. and DeWine, S. (1991) Communication process as target and tool for consultancy intervention: revisiting a hackneyed theme. *Journal of Educational and Psychological Consultation*, 2(4), 303–22.

Day, C., Pope, M. and Denicolo, P. (eds) (1990) *Insight into Teachers' Thinking and Practice*. Basingstoke: Falmer.

Deal, T. and Kennedy, A. (1982) *Corporate Culture*. Reading, MA: Addison-Wesley.

Department for Education (1993) *Code of Practice on the Identification and Assessment of Special Educational Needs*. London: HMSO.

Department for Education (1994a) *Pupil Behaviour and Discipline*. Circular 8/94. London: DFE.

Department for Education (1994b) *The Education of Children with Emotional and Behavioural Difficulties*. Circular 9/94. London: DFE.

Department for Education (1994c) *The Education of Sick Children*. Circular 12/94. London: DFE.

Department of Education and Science (1989) *Discipline in Schools* (The Elton Report). London: HMSO.

Department of Education and Science (1990) *Statistics for Schools*. London: HMSO.

De Shazer, S. (1982) *Patterns of Brief Family Therapy. An Ecosystemic Approach*. New York: Guildford Press.

Dessent, T. (1988) Adapting behavioural approaches to the local authority environment. *Educational Psychology in Practice*, 3(4), 24–8.

Dix, T. (1993) Attributing dispositions to children: an interactional analysis of attribution in socialization. *Personality and Social Psychology Bulletin*, 19(5), 633–43.

Dix, T. and Grusec, J. E. (1985) Parent attribution processes in the socialization of children. In I. Sigel (ed.), *Parental Belief Systems: Their Psychological Consequences for Children* (cited in Dix, 1993).

Dix, T., Ruble, D. N. and Zambarano, R. J. (1989) Mothers' implicit theories of discipline: child effects, parent effects, and the attribution process. *Child Development*, 60, 1373–91 (cited in Dix, 1993).

Dowling, E. and Osborne, E. (eds) (1985) *The Family and the School: A Joint Systems Approach to Problems with Children*. London: Routledge and Kegan Paul.

Dowling, E. and Taylor, D. (1989) The clinic goes to school: lessons learned. *Maladjustment and Therapeutic Education*, 7(1), 24–8.

Eiser, R. J. (1978) Interpersonal attributions. In H. Tajfel and

C. Fraser (eds), *Introducing Social Psychology*, Harmondsworth: Penguin.

Elton Report, *see* Department of Education (1989).

Erchul, W. P., Hughes, J. N., Meyers, J., Hichman, J. A. and Braden, J. P. (1992) Dyadic agreement concerning the consultation process and its relationship to outcome. *Journal of Educational and Psychological Consultation*, **3**(2), 119–32.

Figg, J. and Stoker, R. (1989) A school consultation service. A strategy of referral management leading to second order change. *Educational and Child Psychology*, **6**(3), 34–42.

Fine, M. J. and Holt, P. (1983) Intervening with school problems: a family systems perspective. *Psychology in the Schools*, **20**(1), 59–66.

Fiske, S. T. and Taylor, S. E. (1984) *Social Cognition*. New York: Random House.

Fleet, A. and Cambourne, B. (1989) The coding of naturalistic data. *Research in Education*, **41**, 1–15.

Forehand, R., Sturgis, E. T., McMahon, R. J., Aguar, D., Green, K., Wells, K. C. and Beriner, J. (1979) Parent behavioural training to modify child noncompliance. Treatment generalization across time and from home to school. *Behaviour Modification*, **3**(1), 3–25.

Frederickson, N. (1990) Systems approaches in educational psychology. *Journal of Applied Systems Analysis*, **17**, 3–20.

Fry, L. (1980) Behaviour modifications at Lea Green School. *Newsletter of the Association for Behaviour Modification with Children*, **4**(1), 2–19.

Fuchs, D. and Fuchs, L. S. (1992) Limitations of a feel-good approach to consultation. *Journal of Educational and Psychological Consultation*, **3**(2), 93–7.

Fuchs, D., Fuchs, L. S., Dulan, J., Roberts, H. and Fernstrom, P. (1992) Where is the research on consultation effectiveness? *Journal of Educational and Psychological Consultation*, **3**(2), 151–74.

Galvin, P. and Costa, P. (1994) Building better behaved schools: Effective support at the whole school level. In P. Gray, A. Miller and J. Noakes (eds), *Challenging Behaviour in Schools*. London: Routledge.

Galvin, P., Mercer, S. and Costa, P. (1990) *Building a Better Behaved School*. Harlow: Longman.

Georgiades, N. and Phillimore, L. (1975) The myth of the hero innovator and alternative strategies for organizational change. In C. Kiernan and F. P. Woodford (eds), *Behaviour Modification with the Severely Retarded*. Amsterdam: Associated Scientific Publishers.

Gersch, I. S. (1983) Some teachers' reservations about behavioural approaches and a suggested model for overcoming them. *Behavioural Approaches with Children*, 7(4), 29–35.

Gillham, W. (1981) *Problem Behaviour in Secondary Schools*. London: Croom Helm.

Glaser, B. (1978) *Theoretical Sensitivity*. Mill Valley, CA: Sociology Press (cited in Strauss, 1987).

Glaser, B. and Strauss, A. L. (1967) *The Discovery of Grounded Theory*. Chicago: Aldine.

Glatter, R. (ed.) (1989) *Educational Institutions and Their Environments: Managing the Boundaries*. Milton Keynes: Open University Press.

Grace, N. C., Kelley, M. L. and McCain, A. P. (1993) Attribution processes in mother–adolescent conflict. *Journal of Abnormal Child Psychology*, 21(2), 199–211.

Gray, P. and Noakes, J. (1992) Multidisciplinary work. In D. A. Lane and A. Miller (eds), *Child and Adolescent Therapy: A Handbook*. Milton Keynes: Open University Press.

Gray, P. and Noakes, J. (1993) Re-integration of children with challenging behaviours into the mainstream school community. In A. Miller and D. A. Lane (eds), *Silent Conspiracies: Scandals and Successes in the Care and Education of Vulnerable Young People*. Stoke-on-Trent: Trentham Books.

Gray, P., Miller, A. and Noakes, J. (eds) (1994) *Challenging Behaviour in Schools. Teacher Support, Practical Techniques and Policy Development*. London: Routledge.

Gresham, F. M. and Kendall, G. K. (1987) School consultation research: methodological critique and future research directions. *School Psychology Review*, 16, 306–16.

Gupta, R., Stringer, B. and Meakin, A. (1990) A study of the effectiveness of home-based reinforcement in a secondary school. *Educational Psychology in Practice*, 5(4), 197–200.

Gurney, P. (1987) The use of operant techniques to raise self-esteem in maladjusted children. *British Journal of Educational Psychology*, 57, 87–94.

Hammersley, M. (1984) Staffroom news. In A. Hargreaves and P. Woods (eds), *Classrooms and Staffrooms*. Milton Keynes: Open University Press.

Hammersley, M. and Atkinson, P. (1983) *Ethnography: Principles in Practice*. London: Routledge.

Hanko, G. (1990) *Special Needs in Ordinary Classrooms: Supporting Teachers* (2nd edition). Oxford: Blackwell.

Hargreaves, A. and Woods, P. (eds) (1984) *Classrooms and Staffrooms. The Sociology of Teachers and Teaching*. Milton Keynes: Open University Press.

Hargreaves, D. H. (1975) *Interpersonal Relations and Education* (revised edition). London: Routledge and Kegan Paul.

Harrop, L. A. (1977) The vanishing problem. *British Association for Behavioural Psychotherapy Bulletin*, **5**(3), 51–5.

Harrop, L. A. (1978a) Behaviour modification in the ordinary school setting. *Journal of the Association of Educational Psychologists*, **4**(7), 3–14.

Harrop, L. A. (1978b) Another gain for the modifiers? *Special Education – Forward Trends*, **5**(4), 15–17.

Harrop, L. A. (1983) *Behaviour Modification in the Classroom*. London: Hodder and Stoughton.

Harrop, L. A. and McNamara, E. (1979) The behavioural workshop for classroom problems. A re-appraisal. *British Journal of In-Service Education*, **1**(1), 47–50.

Harrop, L. A. and Williams, T. (1992) Rewards and punishments in the primary school: pupils' perceptions and teachers' usage. *Educational Psychology in Practice*, **7**(4), 211–15.

Hedderley, R. (1977) Contract based referral system – the way to a community psychological service. *Association of Educational Psychologists Journal*, **5**(4), 15–20.

Henning-Stout, M. and Conoley, J. C. (1988) Influencing district change (quoted in J. C. Conoley and C. W. Conoley, 1990).

Henwood, K. L. and Pidgeon, N. F. (1993) Qualitative research and psychological theorizing. In M. Hammersley (ed.), *Social Research, Philosophy, Politics and Practice*. London: Sage.

Hickey, K. A., Imber, S. C. and Ruggiero, E. A. (1977) Modifying independent work habits of elementary students through parent–teacher involvement and co-operation. *Paper presented at Council for Exceptional Children, 55th annual International Convention*, Atlanta, GA, April 1977 (cited in Barth, 1979).

Houghton, S. J. (1991) Promoting generalization of appropriate behaviour across special and mainstream settings: a case study. *Educational Psychology in Practice*, **7**(1), 49–53.

Hoy, W. K. and Miskel, C. G. (1989) Schools and their external environments. In R. Glatter (ed.), *Educational Institutions and Their Environments*. Milton Keynes: Open University Press.

Hutchinson, S. A. (1988) Education and grounded theory. In R. R. Sherman and R. B. Webb (eds), *Qualitative Research in Education: Focus and Methods*. Lewes: Falmer.

Johnston, C., Patenaude, R. L. and Inman, G. A. (1992) Attributions for hyperactive and aggressive child behaviours. *Social Cognition*, **10**(3), 255–70.

Jones, N. and Frederickson, N. (eds) (1990) *Refocussing Educational Psychology*. Basingstoke: Falmer.

Karraker, R. (1972) Increasing academic performance through home managed contingency programs. *Journal of School Psychology*, **10**(2), 173–9 (cited in Barth, 1979).

Kolvin, I., Garside, R. G., Nicol, A. R., Macmillan, A., Wolstenholme, F. and Leitch, I. M. (1981) *Help Starts Here. The Maladjusted Child in the Ordinary School*. London: Tavistock Publications.

Lane, D. A. (1977) Aspects of the use of behaviour modification in secondary schools. *British Association for Behavioural Psychotherapy Bulletin*, **5**(3), 76–9.

Lane, D. A. (1990) *The Impossible Child*. Stoke-on-Trent: Trentham Books.

Lane, D. A. (1994) Supporting effective responses to challenging behaviour: from theory to practice. In P. Gray, A. Miller and J. Noakes (eds), *Challenging Behaviour in Schools*. London: Routledge.

Leach, D. J. (1981) Innovating behaviour-based practice in schools. *Association of Educational Psychologists Journal*, **5**(7), 23–31.

Leach, D. J. and Byrne, M. K. (1986) Some 'spill-over' effects of a home-based reinforcement programme in a secondary school. *Educational Psychology*, **6**(3), 265–76.

Leach, D. J. and Ralph, A. (1986) Home-based reinforcement: a case study. *Behaviour Change*, **3**(1), 58–62.

Leadbetter J., Rose, L. and Tee, G. (1992) Whole-school approaches to reducing problem behaviour. In G. Lindsay and A. Miller (eds), *Psychological Services for Primary Schools*. Harlow: Longman.

Lieberman, A. (ed.) (1990) *Schools as Collaborative Cultures: Creating the Future Now*. Basingstoke: Falmer.

Lieberman, A. and Miller, L. (1990) The social realities of teaching. In A. Lieberman (ed.), *Schools as Collaborative Cultures*. Basingstoke: Falmer.

Little, J. W. (1990) Teachers as colleagues. In A. Lieberman (ed.), *Schools as Collaborative Cultures*. Basingstoke: Falmer.

Long, M. (1988) Goodbye behaviour units, hello support services. *Educational Psychology in Practice*, **4**(1), 17–23.

Lortie, D. (1975) *Schoolteacher. A Sociological Study*. Chicago University Press.

MacDonald, W., Gallimore, R. and MacDonald, G. (1970) Contingency counselling by school personnel: an economical model of intervention. *Journal of Applied Behaviour Analysis*, **3**, 175–82 (cited in Barth, 1979).

McGee, R., Silva, P. A. and Williams, S. (1983) Parents' and teachers' perceptions of behaviour problems in seven-year-old children. *The Exceptional Child*, **30**(2), 151–61.

McMahon, R. J. and Davies, G. R. (1980) A behavioural training program and its side effects on classroom behaviour. *BC Journal of Special Education*, **4**(2), 165–74.

McNamara, E. (1977) Results and impressions of using behaviour modification in a psychological service. *British Association for Behavioural Psychotherapy Bulletin*, **5**(3), 55–62.

McNamara, E. (1979) The use of self-recording in behaviour modification in a secondary school. *Behavioural Psychotherapy*, **7**, 57–65.

McNamara, E. (1982a) Reality problems in classroom research. *Occasional Papers of the DECP*, **6**(2), 50–3.

McNamara, E. (1982b) The misapplication of contingency management in a primary school classroom: a case study. *Behavioural Approaches with Children*, **6**(2), 13–9.

McNamara, E. (1988) Behavioural contracting with secondary aged pupils. *Educational Psychology in Practice*, **2**(4), 21–6.

McNamara, E. and Harrop, L. A. (1979) Behaviour modification in secondary schools – a cautionary tale. *Occasional Papers of the DECP* **3**(2), 38–40.

McNamara, E. and Harrop, L. A. (1981) Behaviour modification in the secondary school: a rejoinder to Wheldall and Austin. *Occasional Papers of the DECP*, **5**(2), 60–3.

McNamara, E. and Heard, C. (1976) Self-control by self-recording. *Special Education – Forward Trends*, **3**, 21–3.

Madsen, C. H., Becker, W. C. and Thomas, D. R. (1968) Rules, praise and ignoring: elements of elementary classroom control. *Journal of Applied Behavioural Analysis*, **1**(2), 139–50.

Merrett, F. (1981) Studies in behaviour modification in British educational settings. *Educational Psychology*, **1**(1), 13–38.

Merrett, F. and Blundell, D. (1982) Self-recording as a means of improving behaviour in the secondary school. *Educational Psychology*, **2**, 147–57.

Merrett, F. and Wheldall, K. (1978) Playing the game: a behavioural approach to classroom management in the junior school. *Educational Review*, **30**(1), 41–50.

Merrett, F. and Wheldall, K. (1987) Natural rates of teacher approval and disapproval in British primary school classrooms. *British Journal of Educational Psychology*, **57**, 95–103.

Miller, A. (1980) Systems theory applied to the work of the educational psychologist. *Association of Educational Psychologists Journal*, **5**(3), 11–15.

Miller, A. (1989a) Behavioural approaches and classroom realities: how educational psychologists and teachers devise and implement behavioural interventions. In K. Reid (ed.), *Helping Troubled Pupils in Secondary Schools*, Volume 2. Oxford: Blackwell.

Miller, A. (1989b) Paradigms losts: What theory informs educational psychologists in their use of behavioural approaches? *Educational Psychology in Practice*, 5(3), 143–7.

Miller, A. (1994a) Successful interventions with problem pupil behaviour in primary schools. A critique of consultative practice between educational psychologists and teachers from the perspectives of applied behaviour analysis, organizational dynamics and attribution shift. (Unpublished PhD. thesis) University of Sheffield.

Miller, A. (1994b) Staff culture, boundary maintenance and successful behavioural interventions in primary schools. *Research Papers in Education*, 9(1), 31–51.

Miller, A. (1994c) Parents and difficult behaviour: always the problem or part of the solution? In P. Gray, A. Miller and J. Noakes (eds), *Challenging Behaviour in Schools*. Milton Keynes: Open University Press.

Miller, A. (1994d) Mainstream teachers talking about successful behaviour support. In P. Gray, A. Miller and J. Noakes (eds), *Challenging Behaviour in Schools*. Milton Keynes: Open University Press.

Miller, A. (1995a) Building grounded theory within educational psychology practice. *Educational and Child Psychology*, 12(2), 5–14.

Miller, A. (1995b) Teachers' attributions of causality, control and responsibility in respect of difficult pupil behaviour and its successful management. *Educational Psychology*, 15, 457–71.

Miller, A. (1996) But what about the others? Teachers' experiences of the impact of individual behavioural interventions on other class members. *Educational Psychology in Practice*, 11(4), 30–4.

Miller, A., Jewell, T., Booth, S. and Robson, D. (1985) Delivering educational programmes to slow learners. *Educational Psychology in Practice*, 1(3), 99–104.

Miller, E. J. (ed.) (1976) *Task and Organization*. Chichester: Wiley.

Morgan, G. (1986) *Images of Organizations*. London: Sage.

Mortimore, P., Sammons, P., Stoll, L., Lewis, D. and Ecob, R. (1984) *School Matters*. Wells: Open Books.

Nias, J. (1985) Reference groups in primary teaching. In S. J. Ball and I. F. Goodson (eds), *Teachers' Lives and Careers*. Lewes: Falmer.

O'Dell, S. (1974) Training parents in behaviour modification. A review. *Psychological Bulletin*, **81**, 418–33.

Osborne, E. (1983) The teacher's relationship with the pupils' families. In I. Salzbergber-Wittenberg, G. Henry and E. Osborne (eds), *The Emotional Experience of Learning and Teaching*. London: Routledge.

Palazzoli, S. M., Cecchin, G., Prata, G. and Boscolo, L. (1978) *Paradox and Counter Paradox: A New Model of the Family in Schizophrenic Transaction*. London: Jason Aronson.

Panagopoulou-Stamatelatou, A. (1990) The use of self-management in primary school settings: a review. *Educational Psychology*, **10**(3), 207–24.

Power, M. J., Benn, R. T. and Morris, J. N. (1967) Delinquent schools? *New Society*, 19 October 1967.

Power, M. J., Benn, R. T. and Morris, J. N. (1972) Neighbourhood, school and juveniles before the courts. *British Journal of Criminology*, April, 111–32.

Power, T. and Bartholomew, K. (1985) Getting uncaught in the middle: a case study in family–school system consultation. *School Psychology Review*, **14**(2), 222–9.

Presland, J. (1972) Helping the maladjusted child. *Journal and Newsletter of the Association of Educational Psychologists*, **3**(2), 31–40.

Presland, J. (1973a) Dealing with disturbing behaviour in the classroom. *Journal of the Association of Educational Psychologists*, **3**(3), 28–32.

Presland, J. (1973b) Helpers for disturbing children. *Journal of the Association of Educational Psychologists*, **3**(4), 36–9.

Presland, J. (1974) Modifying behaviour now. *Special Education – Forward Trends*, **1**(3), 20–2.

Presland, J. (1975) Advising on school behaviour modification. Some practical problems. *Association of Educational Psychologists Journal*, **3**(9), 5–9.

Presland, J. (1977) Behaviour modification in day ESN(M) schools. *Association of Educational Psychologists Journal*, **3**(9), 5–9.

Presland, J. (1978) Teachers' reactions to behaviour modification workshops. *Occasional Papers of the DECP*, **2**(1), 13–19.

Presland, J. (1981) Modifying behaviour long-term and sideways. *Association of Educational Psychologists Journal*, **5**(6), 27–30.

Quicke, J. C. (1978) The professional knowledge of educational psychologists. *Association of Educational Psychologists Journal*, **4**(9), 8–16.

Quicke, J. C. (1982) *The Cautious Expert. A Social Analysis of*

Developments in the Practice of Educational Psychology. Milton Keynes: Open University Press.

Rennie, E. N. F. (1980) Good behaviour games with a whole class. *Remedial Education,* **15,** 187–90.

Reynolds, D. (1992) School effectiveness and school improvement: an updated review of the British literature. In D. Reynolds and P. Cuttance (eds), *School Effectiveness: Research, Policy and Practice.* London: Cassell.

Rice, A. K. (1976) Individual, group and inter-group processes. In E. J. Miller (ed.), *Task and Organization.* Chichester: Wiley.

Rogers, W. (1990) *You Know the Fair Rule.* Harlow: Longman.

Rutter, M., Tizard, J. and Whitmore, K. (1970) *Education, Health and Behaviour.* London: Longman.

Rutter, M., Maughan, B., Mortimore, P. and Ouston, J. (1979) *Fifteen Thousand Hours.* Wells: Open Books.

Safran, J. S. (1991) Communication in collaboration/consultation: effective practices in schools. *Journal of Educational and Psychological Consultation,* **2**(4), 371–86.

Safran, S. P. (1991) The communication process and school-based consultation: what does the research say? *Journal of Educational and Psychological Consultation,* **2**(4), 343–70.

Schein, E. H. (1988) *Process Consultation,* Volume 1 (2nd edition). Reading, MA: Addison-Wesley.

Schweiso, J. J. (1985) Proven effectiveness: assessing the outcomes of interventions. *Behavioural Approaches with Children,* **8**(4), 118–26.

Sharp, R. and Green, A. (1975) *Education and Social Control. A Study in Progressive Primary Education.* London: Routledge and Kegan Paul.

Sheridan, S. M. and Kratochwill, T. R. (1992) Behavioural parent–teacher consultation: conceptual and reseach considerations. *Journal of School Psychology,* **30,** 117–39.

Stratford, R. J. (1990) Creating a positive school ethos. *Educational Psychology in Practice,* **5**(4), 183–91.

Stratford, R. J. and Cameron, R. J. (1979) Aiming at larger targets. *Occasional Papers of the Division of Educational and Child Psychology,* **3**(2), 47–59.

Strauss, A. L. (1987) *Qualitative Analysis for Social Scientists.* Cambridge: Cambridge University Press.

Strauss, A. L. and Corbin, J. (1990) *Basics of Qualitative Research: Grounded Theory Procedures and Techniques.* London: Sage.

Stringer, P., Stow, L., Hibbert, K., Powell, J. and Louw, E. (1992) Establishing staff consultation groups in schools. *Educational Psychology in Practice,* **8**(2), 87–96.

Taylor, A. (1981) New business as usual. Teacher consultation within a contract based system of school visiting. Where do we go from here? *Association of Educational Psychologists Journal*, **5**(5), 57–9.

Taylor, D. (1982) Family consultation in a school setting. *Journal of Adolescence*, **5**, 367–77.

Tempest, A., Huxtable, M. and Knapman, N. (1987) Support and advisory groups: a new initiative in service delivery. *Educational and Child Psychology*, **4**(3), 66–73.

Tindal, G., Parker, R. and Hasbrouck, J. E. (1992) The construct validity of stages and activities in the consultation process. *Journal of Educational and Psychological Consultation*, **3**(2), 99–118.

Tizard, B., Blatchford, P., Burke, J., Farquar, C. and Plewis, I. (1988) *Young Children at School in the Inner City*. Hove: Lawrence Erlbaum Associates.

Topping, K. J. (1983) *Educational Systems for Disruptive Adolescents*. Beckenham: Croom Helm.

Topping, K. J. (1985) Consultative enhancement of school-based action. In D. P. Tattum (ed.), *Management of Disruptive Behaviour in Schools*. Chichester: Wiley.

Tsoi, M. M. and Yule, W. (1976) The effects of group reinforcement in classroom behaviour modification. *Educational Studies*, **2**, 129–40.

Tucker, B. S. and Dyson, E. (1976) The family and the school: utilizing human resources to promote learning. *Family Process*, **15**, 125–41.

Turner, B. (1992) Looking closely and creating grounded theory. Paper presented at ESRC Research Seminar, University of Warwick, 5 March 1992.

Upton, G. and Cooper, P. (1990) A new perspective on behaviour problems in schools: the ecosystemic approach. *Maladjustment and Therapeutic Education*, **8**(1), 3–18.

Wagner, A. C. (1987) 'Knots' in teacher's thinking. In J. Calderhead (ed.), *Exploring Teachers' Thinking*. London: Cassell.

Ward, J. (1971) Modification of deviant classroom behaviour. *British Journal of Educational Psychology*, **41**, 304–13.

Ward, J. (1976) Behaviour modification in education: an overview and model for programme implementation. *Bulletin of the British Psychological Society*, **29**, 257–68.

Weiner, B. (1980) A cognitive–attribution–emotion–action model of motivated behaviour: an analysis of judgements of help-giving. *Journal of Personality and Social Psychology*, **39**, 186–200.

West, J. F. and Idol, L. (1987) School consultation (Part 1): an interdisciplinary perspective on theory, models, and research. *Journal of Learning Disabilities*, **20**(7), 388–408.

Westmacott, E. V. S. and Cameron, R. J. (1981) *Behaviour Can Change*. London: Macmillan.

Wheldall, K. (1981) 'A' before 'C' or the use of behavioural ecology in the classrooms. In P. Gurney (ed.), *Behaviour Modification in Education. Perspectives 5*. University of Exeter.

Wheldall, K. (ed.) (1987) *The Behaviourist in the Classroom*. London: Allen and Unwin.

Wheldall, K. and Austin, R. (1981) Successful behaviour modification in the secondary school: a reply to McNamara and Harrop. *Occasional Papers of the DECP*, **4**(3), 3–8.

Wheldall, K. and Congreave, S. (1980) The attitudes of British teachers towards behaviour modification. *Educational Review*, **32**(1), 53–65.

Wheldall, K. and Glynn, T. (1988) Contingencies in context: a behavioural interactionist perspective in education. *Educational Psychology*, **8**, 5–19.

Wheldall, K. and Merrett, F. (1984) *Positive Teaching. The Behavioural Approach*. London: Unwin Education.

Wheldall, K. and Merrett, F. (1985) *The Behavioural Approach to Teaching Package*. Birmingham: Positive Products.

Wheldall, K. and Merrett, F. (1988) Which classroom behaviours do primary school teachers say they find most troublesome? *Educational Review*, **40**(1), 13–27.

Wheldall, K., Morris, M., Vaughn, P. and Ng, Y. Y. (1981) Rows versus tables: an example of the use of behavioural ecology in two classes of 11-year-old children. *Educational Psychology*, **1**(2), 171–84.

Winnet, R. A. and Winkler, R. C. (1972) Current behaviour modification in the classroom: be still, be quiet, be docile. *Journal of Applied Behaviour Analysis*, **8**, 259–62.

Winter, S. (1981) A behavioural approach to a four-year-old child's restless behaviour. *Behavioural Approaches with Children*, **5**(3), 18–24.

Winter, S. (1983a) Cultivating the caregivers: promoting commitment to the behavioural approach (Part 1). *Behavioural Approaches with Children*, **6**(4), 31–2.

Winter, S. (1983b) Cultivating the caregivers: promoting commitment to the behavioural approach (Part 2). *Behavioural Approaches with Children*, **7**(1), 33–43.

Woods, P. (1984) The meaning of staffroom humour. In A. Hargreaves and P. Woods (eds), *Classrooms and Staffrooms*. Milton Keynes: Open University Press.

Name index

Subject index